# CCAR Journal
## The Reform Jewish Quarterly

# Contents

CONTENTS

# At the Gates — בִּשְׁעָרִים

House Stark was not the first to dread winter's coming. According to the Talmud, Adam originated this fear; as autumn passed and the winter solstice approached, he lamented: "Woe to me! On account of my sins the world is darkening around me."[1] In the winter, warns the Tur,[2] our *yetzer* rebels when we try to leave our beds for prayer. "How can you arise in the morning during this great cold season?" it demands. Fevers are worse in the winter;[3] tossed corn and nuts will delight a wedding couple in summer but sicken them in winter;[4] even a radish, which possesses medicinal properties much of the year, turns deadly during the winter months.[5]

Winter is coming, yes. But so is this first *CCAR Journal* of the year 2022, and it is altogether enchanting. Take comfort, my friends.

Our articles this month are a marvelous, dazzling, and eclectic mix. Philip Graubart sets the perfect tone with his captivating "Notes from the Narrow Place"—revisiting the confinement of the past years with deep and inspiring insight. Our next article—"Sperm Donation and Surrogacy in the Time When the Judges Judged"—may bear the most unexpected and fascinating title in *CCAR Journal* history; and David Zucker's scholarship and wisdom, as ever, does not disappoint. Although written independently of one another, Judith Schindler's meticulously researched and thought-provoking "Cancel Culture, Billy Graham, and the Jews: Weighing Nearly Forty-Five Years of a Historical Record" and debut *Journal* author Neil Hirsch's superbly analyzed and earnestly written "On Accountability and *T'shuvah*: Two Talmudic Stories of Ostracism" are both rooted in history and text—but also guide us as we wrestle with how to draw boundaries, when to exclude, and when—and why, and how—to atone and forgive.

Two important articles on the state of Reform Judaism come next. In a much-anticipated follow-up to the fall 2018 *CCAR Journal* theme issue on the Reform Pay Equity Initiative, Savannah Noray offers an updated data narrative on our Movement's gender wage gap—gratifyingly revealing where our efforts have borne fruit, but also illuminating how much work is left to do. Michael Rosen and David Ellenson also examine the development, progress, and maturation of the Reform Movement in Israel—brilliantly employing as their source the new Israeli Reform/Progressive siddur *T'filat HaAdam*.

Our selection of articles concludes with two meditations on the greatest of issues: our relationship with the Divine and our longing to feel God's presence and grace. Adam D. Fisher beautifully offers spiritual guidance and uplift in "Experiencing God's Care," while Paul Menitoff draws upon scholarship and personal experience to incorporate Spinoza's pantheism, Kaplan's naturalism, and Buber's existentialism into a new, engaging, and meaningful theology. "Isaac and Iphigenia," our final article, is my own; all I can say is that I hope you will like it!

Book reviews continue to be an ever-more important aspect of the *Journal*—as we see in this issue's outstanding analyses of *Plunder: A Memoir of Family Property and Nazi Treasure, A Rooster for Asklepios* and *A Bull for Pluto, The Jews Should Keep Quiet, Bait Shlishi, Shake and Tremor,* and *Nahum, Habakkuk, and Zephaniah: Lights in the Valley.* We are grateful for our talented reviewers and are always ready to work with new ones; please do reach out to me anytime to learn more and—perhaps—to try your hand at writing a review of your own.

Glancing at the cover or the table of contents, you may have noticed that this issue's poetry section is more robust than ever— which is saying a lot! We are proud to present a wonderful cluster of new poems from some of our beloved and familiar *Journal* authors, as well as important emerging voices. In expanding our understanding of what constitutes "Jewish poetry," we have been blessed to publish unique and amazing work—and to receive, from one of our poets, "heartfelt thanks . . . for encouraging me to become a Jewish poet, not just a poet who happens to be Jewish."

*****

Winter was also the season in which the prophet Elijah visited Akiva and Rachel, and she charged her husband to go study Torah.[6] It was the season in which Esther was told she would ascend to the throne of Persia[7] and save her people, the season of Hillel's rescue from the snowy skylight atop the academy of Shemaia and Avtalion.[8] It is the season for spicy and sizzling food,[9] for honey and wine,[10] for hot baths[11] and fragrant oil.[12] It is the season for cozying up with this very special issue of the *CCAR Journal* and warming yourself with the words and the light of our colleagues and friends.

Winter is coming! Enjoy.

Elaine Rose Glickman, Editor

## Notes

1. *Avodah Zarah* 8a.
2. In *Orach Chaim* 1.
3. *Yoma* 29a.
4. *Mishneh Torah, B'rachot* 7:9.
5. *Eiruvin* 56a.
6. *N'darim* 50a.
7. *M'gillah* 13a.
8. *Yoma* 35b.
9 . *Mishneh Torah,* Human Dispositions 4:8.
10, *Mishneh Torah,* Human Dispositions 4:12.
11. *Mishneh Torah,* Human Dispositions 4:16.
12. *Mishneh Torah,* Human Dispositions 4:17.

*Articles*

# Notes from the Narrow Place: A Theological Reflection on Confinement

*Rabbi Philip Graubart*

### Field Trip

Last November, roughly nine months into the pandemic, I was talking to my high school Jewish Philosophy class about seals. Half the students stared at me through computer screens—or I should say, they stared at their screens; I have no idea what they were actually looking at. The other half, those present and in person, wore masks, which effectively hid their boredom (or fascination or disgust) and muffled their voices. My double mask muffled my voice, and vapors from my breath fogged up my glasses. I was using a local dispute over a seal incursion at La Jolla Cove to illustrate the tension between humans and nature. Normally, I told the students, we'd take a field trip to the beach, watch the seals, talk to the people swimming with them and to the protestors urging humans to stay away. Maybe wade into the water ourselves. But this year, I said, of course that's out of the question. Instead we'll . . .

Massive whining ensued, howls of protest, slamming of books, tossing of pens. Not so unusual for teenagers, even high school seniors. But even through my fogged-up lenses, even through their muted screens, their reactions seemed exaggerated. It wasn't as if these coastal San Diego students had been denied trips to the beach in their lives. "We can never do anything," one outraged Yale-bound young man complained, holding on to his mask, so it wouldn't slip off his nose. "Everywhere is off limits. Everything!"

PHILIP GRAUBART is a rabbi and writer living in San Diego, California. His latest novel is *Women and God*.

He sounded like a spoiled five-year-old, but I nodded. I got it. I agreed. The canceled La Jolla beach field trip was a kind of a microcosm of their pandemic year. Beyond the fear, and the illness, and the unspeakable losses, there was the sheer wall of limits, the narrowing of experience, the constriction of possibilities and of choice that defined this year for them and for all of us. All those things we could no longer do: visit friends, shake hands, eat at restaurants, play basketball, touch, hug, flirt, skip school and head to Coachella, stand close to a teacher while she explains something, lighten up a boring class with a field trip. Narrowness defined the pandemic for all of us, but somehow I felt it was worse for high school kids. Their immediate pre-COVID lives were characterized more by possibilities than reality. A high school senior spends a year on the cusp, a year contemplating new potential, new personas, new horizons. Bursting free defines their sensibilities. "Where will I go?" they wonder constantly, allowing themselves to dream more than they ever will in their lives. "Who will I be?" Their reality shifted in one week in March from a life suffused with potential to one defined by what they could not do.

### The Narrow Place

A single line from Psalms went through my mind as I was disappointing my class of sad teens: *Min ha'meitzar karati Yah, anani b'merchav Yah.* ("Out of the narrow place, I call to God. God answers me from the expanses.") We're all in the narrow place, I thought, yearning for the expanses. That night I looked up the psalm—it's 118, verse 5—and discovered some commentary that eventually shifted my own theology, the way I think about God from my own experiences and my own particular circumstances. Two medieval commentaries—Radak and Ibn Ezra—point out that the word for God in the line (*Yah*) is made up of exactly half the letters of God's full name (*YHVH*). It's as if when I'm stuck in the narrow place, I only have access to half of God. The constriction in my possibilities includes my spiritual potential. It's cut off. Halved.

But the Psalmist also uses the word *Yah* in the second half of the verse, where God answers from the *merchav* (the wide place, the place of expansion). The message seems to be that I can find as much of God in the narrowest of places, stricken with the worst physical and spiritual paralysis, as I can in the land of freedom and possibility. "Half of God is enough for the world," Radak writes. The point is that no matter how constricted your life, how narrow the prison cell, how debilitating your disease, spiritual resources glimmer from the walls of the jailhouse—available, sufficient, and possibly healing. When it comes to God's help in the narrow place, the trick is not seeing the glass as half full. It's finding the fullness in what's really half empty.

The Hebrew word I've been translating as "narrow place" is *meitzar*. The root word is *tzar*, meaning "narrow," and it's sometimes translated as "distress" or "sorrow." But just a glance at the letters shows that it's linguistically related to the word *Mitzrayim*, Hebrew for "Egypt." Being in the narrow place is to be thrust back to Egypt, enslaved, confined. But, of course, redemption *begins* in Egypt. Another line from a different psalm (91:15) serves as kind of a response to our call to God from our own private slavery. In a rare case of speaking in God's own voice, the Psalmist writes: "When he [a stricken individual] calls to me, I will answer him. I am with him in his narrowness (*tzarah*). I will rescue him." The prisoner thinks she's calling out to God from behind her prison walls, with her praying flying outwards to Heaven. God responds: No, I'm with you *in Egypt*. Even if I'm only half there, even if I'm barely discernable, I still glimmer toward potential, toward some kind of freedom. I'm not coming to rescue you. I'm already there. The wide places you yearn for are hidden in your prison cell. We'll find them together. You just have work with me, trust that, together, you and I will discover hidden sources of expansiveness. Trust. And wait.

Easier said than done.

## Lungs

### July 2019

Here are some of the things I can no longer do:

Bike.
Play tennis.
Snorkel.
Run.
Eat much of what I enjoy.
Teach.
Work.

Socialize.

Sleep through the night (and often sleep at all).

Breathe, with full confidence.

Asthma is a disease that, among other things, and for mysterious reasons, constricts the lungs. The bronchial tubes narrow, making it harder to breathe. I've suffered with asthma for most of my life. When doctors ask me when it started, I tell them I can't remember; it's always been with me. But for more than fifty years, it was episodic, and fairly well managed through medications. But somehow at age fifty-eight, the inhalers and pills stopped working. Anyone who's dealt with a debilitating chronic illness, a high percentage of the US population, knows what happened next. A year of poking, prodding, tests, tubes through the mouth, through the nose, diets, specialists, drug trials, experimental treatments, IV lines, injections, exhausting flights to consult with additional specialists, tears, despair, alternatives, supplements, restrictions, scoldings, encouragement. Tens of thousands of dollars. Insurance battles, baffling bills. Kind doctors, indifferent doctors, wise doctors, nasty bastard doctors. And no improvement. I remained in my own private Egypt, with constricted lungs, restricted activity, and a narrowing life.

I'm a rabbi, so it might be logical to guess that I called out to God from my narrow place. In fact, like many rabbis I suspect, I dove headfirst into modern, Western biotechnological remedies: pharmaceuticals, CT scans, spirometry, bronchoscopy, FeNO analysis, pH monitoring, echocardiogram. With no regrets. I'd do it again, even though it all came to almost nothing. I put my God side on hold, as if it were a hobby that I'd get back to once the serious stuff was taken care of. It wasn't until a speech pathologist (long story) recommended I try meditation and breathing exercises that my spiritual muscle reemerged. At first it was just a memory of a rabbinical school professor teaching us that God's full name (*YHVH*) sounds like an exhale, like breath—especially the first syllable: *Yah*. And the breathing exercises, controlled inhalation and exhalation, worked—sort of. They didn't cure me, but they provided some fractional relief, and when it comes to breathing, any relief is monumentally significant. Of course it wasn't a cure in the medical sense, because I wasn't adding anything to my body. I was working with the diseased lungs I had. It turned out I could find some healing—a kind of minor redemption—within my own troubled breath. With half a breath. Half of God was still there. *Yah*. I didn't need to call out into the ether from my narrow place. God, a fuller exhale, deeper breaths, was already there.

Or, in non-theological terms, I learned to live with it. When I discovered I could do more with my diseased lungs, with the breath already at hand, I slowly expanded my activities. I started walking with a friend. When he noticed my relatively non-infirm pace, he wondered if I could run. A little. I tried. It didn't seem to damage me physically, and psychologically it made a huge difference. I ran/walked almost every day for a year.

Every once a in a while, I'd glance at my bike, shoved into a corner of the garage. Two months before my fateful asthma attack, I skidded into a rut on the Mission Beach bike bath. I tumbled off the bike, scraped my forehead on the tar, and broke my wrist. After returning home from the emergency room, my wife stored the blood-stained 21-speed bicycle in the garage. For two months I considered repairing it, but chickened out. Then I got sick, and then the pandemic, and bike shops became unavailable. I dreamt of riding. But still I was running. Moving, almost every day.

The next logical step was work. I'd retired early because my life had narrowed to a series of doctor's appointments, tests, and treatments—all in a fog of fatigue and despair. It wasn't just the psychological stress of juggling work and medicine—it was the bone wearying fatigue of keeping it all straight, the professional and the personal—finding substitutes, wrestling insurance forms into coherence, researching treatments, planning pre-school Shabbat dinners, breathlessly leading middle school Israel programs. Altogether, it was too much; so I quit.

But I had something left. At least half a breath. *Yah*. So after a year of early retirement, I asked the school where I'd worked if there was a part-time teaching position available. I was fortunate; there was. In some ways, it was a letdown. I'd been a decision-maker at the school, part of the leadership team, and for the past few decades of my career, I'd either been in charge of an institution, or near the top. Now I was just teaching (just!), and—as a part-time teacher—well out of the circle of decision-makers. But it didn't take long—nor was it a particularly inspired insight—before I discovered that the spiritual expansiveness of a moment teaching a child—face-to-face, even through a screen, even through a mask—matches a lifetime of satisfaction and frustration directing a large institution. I was still in Egypt, too tired for full-time work, too breathless to resume anywhere near my previous level of physical activity. But I'd found width within my narrowed circumstance. I have a name for that previously hidden expansiveness. I call it *Yah*.

## The Narrow Bridge, This Sweet Old World

Shortly after I retired, my sister-in-law took her own life. Carol was one of the most expansive people I knew. A brilliant storyteller, when she held forth on her latest absurd, fascinating case, always a unique study in human frailty and nerve, waving her hands, pointing her thin fingers, winking, smiling slyly, people gathered round, like planets in orbit. The one time I consulted her on a legal case, she spent over two hours with me on the phone, walking me through various choices and scenarios. The next day she sent me a three-thousand-word, tightly argued, yet somehow breezy and funny memo with my options.

She spent wildly on gifts. She gave away thousands of dollars to people she barely knew. When I first met her, she played piano so skillfully, and sang so beautifully, I was sure she was going to pursue a career in music. She played college tennis. I'd played my whole life; she beat me easily. She read voraciously. She was tall, thin, beautiful, talented, funny, intelligent, hugely successful. Strangers fell for her. She killed herself.

How did her full life narrow to a single dark, dense point, a point where, at least for her, she was left with literally only one choice? It's a mystery. The only answer—baffling, unsatisfying—was mental illness. When I spoke at her funeral, I avoided all talk of mental illness, didn't mention the suicide. I spoke about her generosity, her startling capacity to widen her circle of empathy, her glimmering charisma. I didn't touch on the darkness that overwhelmed her. I didn't want to diminish the glow I was conjuring, even for myself, and anyway I had very little to say about it. But as I gathered my memories and considered where illness had led Carol—to her final destination, the place where we'll all end up—I felt a dull ache of familiarity. Limits. Constriction. Options and activities, choices and opportunities that formerly defined me, gradually cut off. One by one. I wasn't suicidal. But I think I knew what it felt like to have the walls close in. To look around at what's left of your life and discover that you're back in Egypt.

When I got home, I put on a song by Lucinda Williams about a friend who'd taken his life. "See what you lost when you left this world," the narrator sings. "Breath from your own lips. The touch of fingertips." She continues with a litany of missed experiences. "The sound of a midnight train. Wearing someone's ring. Someone calling your name . . . this sweet old world." Quotidian. Ordinary. Common. Yet each one a moment of infinite potential, of expansiveness. I had my own litany. *Yah* was with me, here in Egypt, when I twirled my golden wedding ring around my finger, when it reflected the sunlight off its smooth surface into my eyes. When I could hear my own breath, sometimes labored but always steady, always forming the word *Yah*. When my fingers touched someone else's, or even when I caught the sad eyes of a loved one on a computer screen, wondering when we'd see each other again.

"The whole world is a narrow bridge," Rav Nahman, tuberculosis sufferer, taught us. I imagine his breathing came harder than mine, and I certainly have better access to medical care, and a less serious illness. Yet he bequeathed to us an exquisite universe of teachings, wisdom that now expands through space and time. If the whole world really is a very narrow bridge, it means that we're all stuck in the narrow place. We're all back in Egypt. This was certainly true this past pandemic year, when even a two-hour sealgazing field trip to the beach with a bunch of restless, yearning teenagers was out of the question. We survived, those of us who did, by finding grace through Zoom, turning computer screens into open portals, widening the range of spirit and activity, while stuck at home. We also took masked walks and took note of the sweet things in this narrow, old world. Grass, sky, sun, pets, rain. As Radak would say, we made do with half of God, with *Yah*. It was just enough.

In late February, I got my first shot. I celebrated by hauling my bloody, dusty bicycle to a repair shot. Amazingly, the bike endured less damage than I. It was fixed a day later, but I waited. In mid-March, I got my second shot at a Rite Aid pharmacy, not far from my house. Assuming I'd be sick the next day (I was, and for the next two days), I tentatively approached the newly gleaming, good-as-new bike. I hadn't ridden in over two years, since the accident. I held my breath and wheeled the great machine into my driveway.

I twisted my thigh a bit—a pain that would last a week—but I mounted the bicycle. There's a steep downhill incline right outside my house, so I glided a few feet then peddled easily. Wind hit my face. It was a cool day for Southern California. I noticed a young girl I'd never seen riding a tiny white bike, grinning at the breeze, her hair flying through her helmet. A tall neighbor whose name I didn't know waved at me. I saw bushes and workmen and houses and trees. Breath flowed into my body, and out. I felt freer than I had in years.

Of course, this was all downhill. At the bottom, would come exertions, decisions, gravity, limitations. But that was for later. For now, for this blessed moment, I was riding free, taking in the sights, wallowing in the sublime awful beauty of this narrow bridge, this sweet old world.

# Sperm Donation and Surrogacy in the Time When the Judges Judged

*Rabbi David J. Zucker, PhD*

Covering about two hundred years (c. 1200–1000 BCE), the book of Judges mentions twelve charismatic/military leaders, the "judges," who led the tribes against various enemies. Susan Niditch describes Judges as "one of the most exciting portions of the grand traditional history of the people Israel that runs from Genesis through 2 Kings . . . Judges . . . describes a formative and transitional period in the biblical version of Israelite political history."[1] She goes on to describe the book as "a series of narratives, rich in characterization, dramatic tensions, [and] protagonists." In his work on Judges, Marc Z. Brettler describes a pro-Davidic ideology behind the book, that it is essentially a political tract, which argues for the legitimacy of the Davidic kingship.[2] Although the book of Ruth in the Masoretic Text and in Rabbinic tradition is part of the Hagiographa/Writings/*K'tuvim*, it is set at a time "when the Judges judged" (Ruth 1:1) and it provides the background for the lineage that leads to King David.[3] By way of contrast, in the Jewish Hellenistic tradition, for example in the Septuagint, composed circa 250 BCE (and consequently later in the Christian biblical tradition), Ruth is embedded in the Prophets/ *N'vi-im,* just after the book of Judges.

Like Judges, Ruth is rich in characterization, dramatic tensions, and protagonists. The narrative of the events found in Judges 13, leading up to the birth of Samson, have some parallels with the birth of Obed in the book of Ruth. In both instances a woman who

RABBI DAVID J. ZUCKER, PhD (C70) retired in 2011 as director of Chaplaincy Care at Shalom Cares in Aurora, Colorado. His book *American Rabbis: Facts and Fiction,* 2nd ed. (Wipf and Stock, 2019) considers the real American rabbinate and how it is reflected in fiction. He is the author with Moshe Reiss, *z"l,* of *The Matriarchs of Genesis: Seven Women, Five Views* (Wipf and Stock, 2015).

previously was childless now produces progeny, one becomes a great hero (Samson) and the other, the direct ancestor of a great hero (King David). There are intriguing circumstances in each case. In Judges, Manoah's wife twice meets up *alone* with a messenger/angel of God (*malach YHVH*) under some extraordinary circumstances. In chapter 3, on her own, Ruth goes out of her way to encounter Boaz when he is completely by himself. In both cases, Manoah's wife and then Ruth after she marries Boaz, the woman gives birth to a son. In the former case there are strong suggestions of an unacknowledged sperm donation. In the latter case Boaz definitely is the sperm donor, and Ruth serves as a kind of surrogate, providing progeny to continue the line of Elimelech-Naomi of Judah.

### Unacknowledged Sperm Donation: Manoah's Wife and the Man of God

Manoah and his wife are childless. In Judges 13:2 she is termed an *akarah*, a word often translated as "barren," which more properly should be translated as "childless."[4] One day, according to the biblical narrative, one of God's messengers/angels, unexpectedly and without fanfare appears to the wife of Manoah of the tribe of Dan. He tells her that she will conceive and bear a son (or that she is already pregnant, the Hebrew can be translated either way). Niditch proposes that the angel's words "reveal that the woman has conceived and will bear a son."[5] Since the child is to be a Nazirite from birth, the messenger/angel gives her clear instructions for her own conduct and for her future son (no hair cutting, no wine or intoxicants, and no unclean food). The child shall begin to deliver Israel from the Philistine oppression (Judg. 13:3–5). I propose that one way to read the biblical text is that it suggests or at the least *allows* the interpretation that it is the so-called frightening-looking "man of God" (Judg. 13:6) who impregnates Manoah's wife because she and Manoah are unable to have children together. The term used in Judges 13 is *Nazir Elohim*, a phrase not to be found anywhere else in the Bible. It might be translated as "Divine Nazarite" or "Nazarite through the word of God," which should not be identified with the Torahic Nazarite, but rather be understood as an essential quality of that semi-divine offspring that justifies his unique treatment from the first moment of pregnancy to the end of his life.[6]

Such an interpretation presupposes that *at the very least* there are echoes of semi-divine/human sexual intercourse (see comments below, as well as that of Brettler in note 19). There is no doubt that by the time this episode became Scripture those ideas were downplayed. Nonetheless, Everett Fox explains that from "the outset, the story . . . involves secrets and mysteries . . . the narrative is studded with folklore motifs." He also writes that the appearance of an angel announcing an impending birth to "a woman (with an absent husband) . . . [finds a] parallel annunciation account in the New Testament [Luke 1:26–31] . . . and for this and other reasons, Shimshon was often regarded in early and later Christianity as a prefiguring ('type') of Jesus."[7]

While God's messenger appears without any fanfare, this still is an extraordinary event. His presence is in contrast to Manoah, who is systematically marginalized in the text.[8] J. Cheryl Exum has noted that the narrative "dissociate[s] her [Manoah's wife's] pregnancy from the sex act, not even acknowledging it in typical biblical fashion, 'Manoah knew his wife and she conceived.' Rather the story begins with the (male) messenger of Yhwh telling the woman she is pregnant."[9] As Adele Reinhartz explains, "There are . . . hints . . . that the angel may have had some more direct role in the conception of this child than merely announcing it." She goes on to note that there are suggestions in the text of "sexual intimacy between the woman and the angel."[10]

The woman goes to her husband, and reports the essence of the angelic annunciation. She explains that a "man of God" with the appearance of a frightening looking angel *came* to her. She neither asked his name, nor did he self-identify. In the text of the Hebrew Scriptures there is a hint of intrigue. Manoah's wife "comes" (*vatavo*) to her husband. She informs him that a mysterious figure, a *man* of God "came to me" (*ba elai*) (Judg. 13:6). In biblical Hebrew the verb "to come/*lavo*" from the root letters *bet-vav-alef*, often indicates ejaculating (i.e., "coming")—see examples of this verb below. One interpretation is that Manoah's wife is subtly hinting that she has had intercourse with this man of God. Manoah never questions his wife; he seems to accept her statement at face value. She is/will be pregnant. How does Manoah hear her words? He says in Judges 13:8, let the man "come again" (*yavo*) to us. Is Manoah simply saying, let him return, or is he quietly confirming that this man of God impregnated his wife? It is possible that for the received text of the biblical writer there is no sexual inference in either of their words, that *coming* simply means either going or appearing; that these "two 'comings' . . . were but 'appearances' and carry no sexual implication,"[11] but it may be more than that. I submit that the biblical text allows for both interpretations, the literal going/appearing and *also that she knowingly had intercourse with the so-called man of God/God's messenger.* In Judges, Manoah approaches God directly; he seeks divine confirmation as well as guidance as to how to act with the child following his birth. He says, "please let the man of God that you sent *come* to us again and let him instruct us how to act with the child" (Judg. 13:8). God heeds Manoah's request. Shortly thereafter the angel of God makes a second visitation. He reappears/comes to the wife as she is sitting alone in a field. The biblical text is clear, she is alone and *her husband Manoah was not with her* (v. 9). She runs to Manoah and tells him that this special figure has returned: "The man who *came* to me" has reappeared. Manoah joins her and ascertains that this is the same man as before (vv. 9–11). Once again in these verses, the same intriguing verb is used, *vayavo* (v. 9). The phrase actually echoes Abraham's impregnating Hagar (Gen. 16:4, *vayavo el Hagar*), Jacob's impregnating Bilhah (Gen. 30:4, *vayavo eilehah Yaakov*), and Boaz's impregnating Ruth (Ruth 4:13, *vayavo eilehah*); here, *vayavo el . . . ha-ishah* ("he came . . . to the woman"). Finally in verse 24 Manoah's wife gives birth to and names Samson. The biblical scholars Avigdor Shinan and Yair Zakovitch write that there may well be the echo here of an earlier tradition that the uncommonly strong figure Samson was the product of a divine being and a human woman. On each occasion Manoah's wife was there alone, she was without her husband. They explain that these facts, that she was "without her husband awaken our suspicion . . .—if only of the possibility—that something unseemly occurred between the angel and the woman."[12] Shinan and Zakovitch then draw parallels with the Greek myths about the birth of Heracles, the son of the god Zeus and the mortal woman Alcmene. In that story Alcmene's husband is away when Zeus impregnates her.[13]

Manoah is a Danite. Scholars write of the connections between the Philistines, who were a maritime people originating in Greece, and the early Danites.[14] Samson marries a Philistine woman (Judges 14), and although Delilah is not specifically termed a Philistine, Philistines engage her to betray Samson's secret (Judges 16). This echo of Greek myths of a divine/semi-divine sexual relationship with a human woman may well be an example of cross-cultural memory.

When late in the first century CE the Jewish historian Flavius Josephus (ca. 37–100 CE) in his *Judean Antiquities* retells these events, he writes that on an occasion when Manoah's wife "had been left alone, [there] appeared a specter, an angel of God, similar to a *handsome* and tall youth." This messenger brings her "the good news of the forthcoming birth of a son . . . [who] would be *handsome* and famous for his strength."[15] In each case Josephus uses the Greek word *kalos* ("handsome") to describe first the angel and then the future child. These physical descriptions are unique to Josephus; they are not part of the biblical tradition. In *Judean Antiquities* Manoah's wife is "notable for her beauty,"[16] but physical descriptions of Manoah do not appear in Josephus or in the Bible. That the same descriptive word, handsome/*kalos* is used for both the angel and the promised child, I suggest, is Josephus's nod to the tradition of a divine/human parentage for a specially strong hero.

The biblical narrative found in Judges is also reflected in a pseudepigraphic composition, *Pseudo-Philo Biblical Antiquities (Liber Antiquitatum Biblicarum)* (hereafter *Biblical Antiquities*). This work "was almost certainly written between 70 CE and 150 CE." It is "an example of a genre known as rewritten Bible [where the] . . . the author reviews the biblical narrative from Adam to David, adding, subtracting, embellishing, and revising."[17] Though ascribed to Philo, the material here is handled very differently than that of the Alexandrian philosopher of the first century CE. Further, "there are several points at which Pseudo-Philo explicitly contradicts the views of Philo."[18] Like the Bible there are spoken monologues, or dialogues between the characters: Manoah, his wife, and the angel. Matters concerning Samson's birth are presented in chapter 42 and the first verse in chapter 43.

Manoah's response in *Biblical Antiquities* differs greatly from the account in Judges where he appears to accept his wife's statement, although not unreasonably he seeks additional information as to how the family should act. In *Biblical Antiquities* Manoah patently does not believe his wife, who coincidentally is given a name, Eluma. Manoah is disturbed that she, and not he, was given the angelic annunciation. He says, "Am I not worthy to hear the signs and wonders that God has done among us or to see the face of his messenger?" (42:5). Even while he is complaining about this situation, the angel visits Eluma a second time. "The angel of YHWH *came again to* his wife" (42:6–7), where, once again, she is depicted as being *alone* outside in a field, while Manoah is in their house. The angel sends Eluma to fetch Manoah who then comes out to the field (42:6). When there the angel gives him clear directions: "Go into your wife and do all these things." Such advice is only found in *Biblical Antiquities*. With ill grace Manoah replies to the angel, "I am going," he says, "but see to it, sir, that your word be accomplished regarding your servant," to which the angel accedes (42:7). This command, to Manoah, to "go into [his] wife" feels like a subterfuge to have him believe that he will father the child, where actually Eluma has already been impregnated by the angel/messenger. In all three versions of this narrative, in Judges, in Josephus, and in *Biblical Antiquities*, "a barren [childless] woman suddenly became pregnant with no apparent interceding sexual experience."[19] Since in the Hebrew Bible this is impossible, this narrative serves at the very least as an echo of the example of an Unacknowledged Sperm Donor.

### Voluntary Surrogacy/Sperm Donation: Ruth and Boaz

On the surface the book of Ruth appears to be a romantic and idyllic tale, recounting a narrative about a direct ancestor of King David. Yet it also addresses some critical matters regarding the passing on of property rights. A number of underlying issues in the book of Ruth are similar to the narrative of Judah and Tamar in Genesis 38, although in that situation there is both an intended and unintended sperm donation (Tamar intends this to happen, the results are different than Judah had intended). The biblical text in Ruth unambiguously points to this connection, mentioning Tamar explicitly, "May your house be like the house of Perez whom *Tamar* bore to Judah" (Ruth 4:12). In the case of Tamar a woman (probably a Canaanite, her origin is not explained) marries a member of the clan of Judah, but her husband Er (Judah's oldest son) dies, and his next younger brother Onan chooses not to impregnate Tamar (Levirate marriage/*yibbum*). In terms of Ruth who is a Moabite, she marries Mahlon, the son of Elimelech and Naomi of Bethlehem (which is part of the tribe of Judah). Yet before she can become pregnant, Ruth's husband dies as does Mahlon's brother, Chilion.

Consequently there are no direct male heirs to claim the family property back in Bethlehem. Both women, earlier Tamar now Ruth, need to produce a legitimate son who can then be the direct inheritor. In this case in Ruth, it is worth stating that at its essence the legal bases of this narrative matches the Torahic law of yibbum, namely that this procedure is in no way anecdotal but rather it is part of the social order constructed by biblical law.

In the book of Ruth, Boaz marries and impregnates Ruth, who gives birth to Obed. In this sense Boaz's role is that of a sperm donor from the tribe of Judah. In the book, Ruth is praised for her kindness. Yet, as Amy-Jill Levine points out, she consistently is termed Ruth the Moabite. This highlights her foreign, non-Israelite origins. Ruth's Moabite heritage makes her a descendant of the incestuous union of Lot and his daughters (Genesis 19). At the close of the Book of Ruth it is important to note that the text highlights that "the Israelite woman Naomi, not the Moabite Ruth, becomes the acclaimed mother of Obed (4:17)."[20] This action, which focuses on Naomi, to some considerable extent eclipses Ruth's role as mother. Naomi takes charge. "Naomi took the child and held him to her bosom. She became his foster mother, and the *women neighbors gave him a name, saying, 'A son is born to Naomi'*" (Ruth 4:16–17). Ruth produces the desired heir, and now her role is essentially finished. Yes, she may be around and have a role in rearing Obed, similar to the positions of Hagar with Ishmael and Bilhah and Zilpah in terms of Dan and Naphtali (Bilhah and Jacob's sons) and Zilpah with Gad and Asher (Zilpah and Jacob's sons) in Genesis,[21] but in effect she served her purpose. She is the designated surrogate womb, and Boaz is the sperm donor. Vanessa L. Ochs states that Ruth "essentially becomes a surrogate mother . . . [the] townswomen [congratulate Naomi, not Ruth.]. 'God gave *you* a redeemer,' they tell Naomi. 'He will redeem *you*, sustain *you*'" (emphases in original). Unlike most child namings, here it not the usual mother, or sometimes the father who names the child, but the townswomen. "Naomi holds the baby to her bosom, and, figuratively, nurses him, making Ruth utterly unnecessary."[22] Tamara Cohn Eskenazi and Tikvah Frymer-Kensky point out that some "contemporary readers are troubled by the seeming surrogate position to which Ruth is relegated." They challenge this view and argue that "such interpretations go against the grain of the narrative that shows how *hesed* [loving-kindness] triumphs over loss."[23]

I propose that the matter is more complicated. *Chesed* does triumph over loss, but on another level Ruth and Boaz also serve as surrogate and sperm donor to actively perpetuate the Elimelech/Mahlon line. In his Anchor Bible commentary on Ruth, Edward F. Campbell explains that from "the story's point of view, the combination of redemption and levirate marriage is a *presupposition*" (emphasis in original).[24] Levirate marriage/surrogacy/sperm donation are all intertwined with redemption and *chesed*. Referring to the earlier scholarship of Hans Wilhelm Hertzberg (1959), Campbell explains that in Ruth chapter 3 one finds the "repetition of several common words which have potential double meanings." These words include the verb *s-k-b* [*shin-kaf-vet*] "to lie down" which can mean "to have sexual intercourse." Further there "is almost the full range of nuances of the Hebrew term 'to know' [*y-d-a—yud-dalet-ayin,* and the ancient . . .] audience will doubtless have supplied in their own minds one additional frequent meaning, 'to have sexual intercourse with.' Finally, it may be that there is intentional double meaning in the use of the word *ba* [from the root letters *bet-vav-alef*] 'to come (toward), to go into,' which occurs in 3:4, 7, and 14 [author's note: just as in Judges 13 with Manoah's wife] and will reappear with a clear sexual meaning in the crucial verse 4:13 (so Hertzberg)"[25]

## Conclusion

The concepts of sperm donation and surrogacy as practiced in the contemporary world have precedents in the Hebrew Bible. While the examples of Hagar, Bilhah, and Zilpah are the most obvious examples of surrogacy in the Bible, a case can be made that Ruth also serves as a surrogate womb. As the wife of the deceased Mahlon, she provides an heir that allows the Elimelech-Naomi/Mahlon line to continue. Boaz functions as the sperm donor in a way that Onan chose not to fulfill for Tamar. Ruth is in a very different position than Hagar, and Bilhah and Zilpah, who were servants to their mistresses and secondary wives to Abraham and Jacob, respectively. Unlike those women, Ruth has a choice in this matter, and at Naomi's suggestion she willingly approaches Boaz to act as the sperm donor. She proactively seeks him out and asks him to serve as her protector (Ruth 3:6–9). There is no reason to believe, unlike Hagar, and Bilhah and Zilpah, that she will be a grass widow. In Genesis

38 Tamar has to work surreptitiously to achieve her goals. She actively seeks out not only a sperm donor, but a very specific sperm donor, one who will legitimately further the Judahite line. In terms of Manoah's wife, reading Judges 13 as proposed in this article, it appears that that at the very least there is the echo of an older tradition that a woman seeks out, or is sought out, and has intercourse with a sperm donor to resolve the matter of her apparent inability to produce a child with her husband. Life in ancient Israel was very different from life in the twenty-first century. The world of science opens up many possibilities unknown in the past. Sperm donation and surrogacy today take place under different circumstances, and there is legislation addressing these matters. Nonetheless, broadly speaking, both sperm donation and surrogacy have biblical precedents and took place when the judges judged.

## Acknowledgment

Thanks to Alison Benjamin for offering valuable criticisms in an earlier draft.

## Notes

1. Susan Niditch. *Judges: A Commentary*, Old Testament Library (Louisville: Westminster John Knox 2011 [2008]), 1.
2. Niditch, *Judges*, 8. Niditch refers to Marc Z. Brettler's work, *The Book of Judges* (London: Routledge, 2002).
3. Yael Avrahami, "Recasting David's Foreign Origin," https://www.thetorah.com/article/book-of-ruth-recasting-davids-foreign-origins.
4. Nahum M. Sarna, *The JPS Torah Commentary—Genesis* (Philadelphia: Jewish Publication Society, 1989), 87, n. 30. Sarah is termed childless/*akarah* (Gen. 11:30), but she gives birth to Isaac. Rebekah is termed childless/*akarah*, and following an appeal to God, God responds and opens her womb, and she bears Esau and Jacob (Gen. 25:21–26). Rachel is termed childless/*akarah* (Gen. 29:31) but later gives birth to Joseph and Benjamin.
5. Niditch, *Judges*, 143.
6. With appreciation to Dr. Rabbi Yehoyada Amir for suggesting this insight.
7. Everett Fox, *The Early Prophets: Joshua, Judges, Samuel, and Kings. The Schocken Bible*, vol. 2 (New York: Schocken, 2014), 210.
8. Yairah Amit. "Manoah Promptly Followed his Wife (Judges 13.11): On the Place of the Woman in Birth Narratives," in *A Feminist*

*Companion to Judges*, ed. A. Brenner (Sheffield: Sheffield Academic Press, 1993), 147–50. "Manoah takes a secondary role to his wife." J. Cheryl Exum, *Fragmented Women: Feminist (Sub)versions of Biblical Narratives*. (Sheffield: JSOT Supplemental Series 163, 1993), 63.

9. Exum, *Fragmented Women*, 66.

10. Adele Reinhartz. "Samson's Mother: An Unnamed Protagonist," in *A Feminist Companion to Judges*, ed. A. Brenner (Sheffield: Sheffield Academic Press, 1993), 166, 167.

11. Avidgor Shinan and Yair Zakovitch, *From Gods to God: How the Bible Debunked, Suppressed, or Changed Ancient Myths and Legends*, trans. V. Zakovitch (Lincoln: University of Nebraska Press/ Philadelphia: Jewish Publication Society, 2012), 190.

12. Shinan and Zakovitch, *From Gods to God*, 191–92.

13. Shinan and Zakovitch, *From Gods to God*, 195. See also Y. Zakovitch, "The Strange Biography of Samson," in *From Bible to Midrash: Portrayals and Interpretive Practices*, ed. Hanne Trautner-Kromann (Lund: Arcus, 2005), 19–36.

14. It "may be that in pre-Philistine days Dan had itself been a maritime 'tribe.'" Robert G. Boling, *Joshua, Anchor Bible* (New York: Doubleday, 1982), 467; Niditch, *Judges*, 79. https://www.haaretz. com/archaeology/MAGAZINE-tribe-of-dan-sons-of-israel-or-of-greek-mercenaries-hired-by-egypt-1.5468423. Thanks to Ted Stainman for pointing out the Dan-Philistine connection.

15. F. Josephus, *Judean Antiquities* [*The Antiquities of the Jews*]. Silvia Castelli, "The Birth of Samson," in *Outside the Bible: Ancient Jewish Writings Related to Scripture*, vol. 2, ed. Louis H. Feldman, James L. Kugel, and Lawrence H. Schiffman (Philadelphia: Jewish Publication Society, 2013), 1245–46 (5.277).

16. Josephus, *Judean Antiquities*, 1244 (5.276).

17. Howard Jacobson, "Pseudo-Philo, Book of Biblical Antiquities," in *Outside the Bible: Ancient Jewish Writings Related to Scripture*, vol. 1., ed. Louis H. Feldman, James L. Kugel, and Lawrence H. Schiffman (Philadelphia: Jewish Publication Society, 2013), 470. See also D. J. Harrington, "Pseudo-Philo," in *The Old Testament Pseudepigrapha*, vol. 2, ed. James H. Charlesworth (Garden City, NY: Doubleday, 1985), 299. The translation used here is by Howard Jacobson, *A Commentary on Pseudo-Philo's Liber Antiquitatum Biblicarum* (Leiden: Brill, 1996).

18. Harrington, "Pseudo-Philo," 300.

19. Tammi J. Schneider, *Berit Olam: Judges* (Collegeville, MN: Liturgical Press, 2000), 195. See Brettler, who suggests that the "Man of God" is Samson's father. Marc Z. Brettler, "Who Was Samson's Real Father?" (2017), https://thetorah.com/article/who-was-samsons-real-father, and Naphtali Meshel, "Samson the Demigod?" (2019), https://www.thetorah.com/article/samson-the-demigod.

20. Amy-Jill Levine, "Ruth," in *The Women's Bible Commentary*, ed. C. A. Newsom and S. H. Ringe (London: SPCK; Louisville, KY: Westminster John Knox, 1992), 79.

21. See David J. Zucker, "In/Voluntary Surrogacy in Genesis," *The Asbury Journal* 76, no. 1 (2021): 9–24.

22. *"making Ruth utterly unnecessary."* Author's comment: Technically Ruth is pivotal to provide breast milk for Obed, though in principle a wetnurse could have done the same. Vanessa L. Ochs, "Reading Ruth: *Where Are the Women*?" in *Reading Ruth: Contemporary Women Reclaim a Sacred Story*, ed. J. A. Kates and G. T. Reimer (New York: Ballentine, 1994), 296. See also "With the birth of the child, Ruth . . . disappear[s] from the text!" Mona DeKoven Fishbane, "Ruth: Dilemmas of Loyalty and Connection," in *Reading Ruth*, 306.

23. Tamara C. Eskenazi and Tikvah Frymer-Kensky, *Ruth: The Traditional Hebrew Text with the New JPS Translation*, JPS Bible Commentary (Philadelphia: Jewish Publication Society, 2011), 92.

24. Edward F. Campbell, Jr. *Ruth*, Anchor Bible 7 (Garden City, NY: Doubleday, 1975), 132.

25. Campbell, *Ruth*, 131–32.

# Cancel Culture, Billy Graham, and the Jews: Weighing Nearly Forty-Five Years of a Historical Record

*Rabbi Judith Schindler*

Is the Jewish world too quick to write off a leader as antisemitic, akin to when we hastily discard friends or supporters because of an offhand antisemitic comment, a thoughtless repeating of a stereotype? Or do the words of leaders captured in diaries or on private recordings reflect a deeper, more insidious hate to which our Jewish antennae must be keenly and necessarily sensitive? From President Truman's 1947 diary, found in 2003, which claimed that Jewish abuse of power is worse than that of Stalin or Hitler,[1] to President Franklin D. Roosevelt's privately expressed antisemitic sentiments alleging Jewish dominance and inferior Jewish blood,[2] each historian must weigh the evidence and determine the balance of a leader's life work.

Consider the Reverend Billy Graham (1918–2018), one of the most influential evangelical leaders who, over the course of six decades, preached in 185 countries to 215 million people through crusades and broadcasts, and shared messages face-to-face with 77 million people in 70 countries.[3] Graham has a forty-five-year public record of speaking favorably about the Jewish community. He received three awards from national Jewish organizations for using his leadership position to passionately support and defend

RABBI JUDITH SCHINDLER is the Sklut Professor of Jewish Studies and director of the Stan Greenspon Center for Peace and Social Justice at Queens University of Charlotte and rabbi emerita of Temple Beth El in Charlotte, North Carolina. She co-authored *Recharging Judaism: How Civic Engagement is Good for Synagogues, Jews, and America* (CCAR Press, 2018) and was a consulting editor for *Deepening the Dialogue: Jewish-Americans and Israelis Envisioning the Jewish-Democratic State* (CCAR Press, 2019).

the Jewish people. Graham affirmed that as early as his conversion (his spiritual enlightenment and "making his decision for Christ") at the age of seventeen, he, a southerner born in North Carolina, began immediately to wrestle with race and acknowledge "the debt" he "owed to Israel, to Judaism and to the Jewish people." Over the course of four decades he used his power to help the State of Israel, to assist imperiled Jewish individuals and communities, and to preach against missionizing the Jews.[4]

Yet the 2002 release of a recording from a secretly taped February 1972 conversation between Graham, President Nixon (a well-documented antisemite), and Nixon's Chief of Staff, H. R. Haldeman, and the 2009 release of a recorded 1973 phone call between Graham and Nixon, revealed another side of Billy Graham. The Jewish community's faith in this evangelical leader's friendship and allyship was largely shattered when they heard Graham audibly supporting Nixon's 1972 rant against Jewish domination of the media. Graham remarked: "This stranglehold has got to be broken or the country's going down the drain."[5]

Jewish leaders again expressed disillusionment when hearing a recorded February 1973 exchange in which Graham vocally supported another scathing verbal attack by Nixon against the Jews. Graham added his own painfully prejudiced words that the nation's problems can be attributed to those Jews who belong to "the synagogue of Satan."[6]

Despite his nearly lifelong commitment to support and protect Jews globally in their times of peril by intervening at the highest levels of political leadership at critical moments when the safety and security of the Jewish people and Israel had been in jeopardy, many Jewish leaders were quick to "cancel" Graham. This renunciation by Jewish leadership failed to credit Graham for preaching a philosemitic theology, working to support the safety of Jews behind the Iron Curtain, publicly proclaiming his opposition to proselytizing Jews, and advocating support for the State of Israel from 1967 forward. Of greatest import, was Graham's impassioned intervention with Nixon during the Yom Kippur War that led to an immediate US lifesaving airlift of more than 22,000 tons of tanks, artillery, and supplies from October 14 to November 14, 1973.[7]

In the spirit of fairmindedness and out of a need to maintain important alliances, the archives recording forty-five years of Graham's actions and writings warrant reopening. They present compelling evidence for reevaluating Graham's record. For twenty-three years, from 1969 until his death in 1992, Rabbi Marc Tanenbaum, in his role as national director of interreligious affairs of the American Jewish Committee (AJC), maintained a continued correspondence and friendship with Graham.[8] As the Jewish-evangelical relationship was part of Tanenbaum's professional portfolio, the rabbi was thorough in archiving Graham's articles, letters, and speeches on all topics related to Judaism. Sometimes at Tanenbaum's urging and often other times completely of his own accord, Graham took risks to stand with and for the Jewish community and Israel on both the national and international stage.

In our current cancel culture, society is quick to publicly shame and silence individuals who are perceived to have committed a social transgression. But if Jewish communal leaders seek to build valuable bridges of support with today's evangelical community, we would benefit from delving more deeply into Graham's historical record to assess his character and his achievements insofar as they have benefitted Jews and Israel.

## Graham's Influence and Impact Safeguarding the Jewish People

Graham's forty-five-year support of Israel and the Jewish people, as an evangelical leader of unmatched influence, was remarkable. As early as 1966, Graham's voice emerged as a beacon in Jewish-Christian relations. In his opening address at the World Congress on Evangelism in West Berlin (where one Arab Christian expressed the belief that Jews were gathered in Israel so as to bring about their end in one blow fulfilling a prophecy of Gog and Magog that will mark the end of time and dawn of a messianic age), Graham's voice stood out with a clear declaration of appreciation for the Jewish foundations of Christianity and with a call to accountability for Christianity's historic sins against them. "Of the Jewish people we ask forgiveness," he preached, and then made clear: "We must remember that our Savior was born of a Jewish mother, and it is to this people that we owe the Bible."[9] Graham traced his strong appreciation for Judaism back to his conversion—his acceptance of his own personal relationship with and responsibility to Jesus.[10]

During a ten-day Billy Graham Crusade at Madison Square Garden, on June 23, 1969, the evangelical leader accepted an invitation by the American Jewish Committee (AJC) to his first formal meeting with American Jewish leadership. After AJC's success with methodical and ongoing advocacy with American Catholic leadership leading to *Nostra Aetate*, the AJC recognized the potential powerful benefit of developing a relationship of depth with the evangelical community. The Graham meeting with approximately thirty Jewish religious and community leaders, including rabbinical representatives of the Reform, Conservative, and Orthodox movements, grew out of AJC's preparation for an August 1969 National Baptist-Jewish Scholars Conference at the Southern Baptist Theological Seminary in Louisville, Kentucky.[11] The "genuine feel of rapport" reported by Jewish delegates present at that initial meeting would mark the beginning of a three-and-a-half decade relationship of correspondence, private meetings, and formal conferences and ceremonies connecting Graham to the Jewish community.

Graham's theology rejected replacement theology; he taught instead that Christians do not displace Jews nor are Jews rejected by God or cursed. The Jewish denial of Jesus, Graham posited, allowed for gentiles to be included in the covenant and to "be grafted on to the Jewish people" (an image emerging from Romans 11) thus sharing with them God's blessings. Graham soundly rejected claims of Jewish deicide by declaring: "The Romans killed Christ." And then he underscored his meaning, "All of the people of that day had a part in the tragedy. It was man's sin as man that was responsible, not the sin of man as Jew or as Gentile."[12]

Graham's scholarship affirmed the Hebrew Bible as the foundation of Christian Scripture. In Graham's introduction to Leonard Yaseen's 1985 book *The Jesus Connection: To Triumph Over Anti-Semitism*, Graham wrote: "Evangelical Christians especially have an affinity for the Jews because the Bible they love is essentially a Jewish book written under the influence of God's Spirit. One theologian has said: 'Remove the New Testament books written by the Jews and only two remain, Luke and Acts. Remove every Jewish concept, every Jewish influence from the New Testament and only a question here and there from a pagan source is left, scarcely enough for one short paragraph.'"[13]

Graham's leadership rejected the proselytization of the Jewish people. This became especially important in response to two evangelical efforts in the early 1970s that elicited waves of pressing concern in the American Jewish community that Jews would be targeted for proselytization. The first was Explo '72, an International Student Congress on Evangelism sponsored by Campus Crusade for Christ, which brought 75,000 Christian students (mostly high school and college) to Dallas for a week of training on evangelism during the day and concerts at night. It was referred to as a "religious Woodstock" and named Explo for the spiritual explosion it aimed to create.[14]

The second event evoking even greater Jewish distress was Key '73—a unified effort of more than 150 denominations "to share with every person in North America more fully and more forcefully the claims and message of Jesus Christ." Evangelical events were planned throughout the 1973 calendar year.

The rising national Jewish anxiety surrounding the Key '73 campaign, and reports over the psychological harassment carried out by young evangelists on high school and college campuses, compelled Graham to invite Tanenbaum to his mountaintop home in Montreat, North Carolina. The two men—one an internationally prominent evangelical leader and the other the national director of interreligious affairs of the AJC—met on February 27, 1973, engaging in a three-hour discussion on a broad range of Jewish and universal concerns. Following that meeting, Tanenbaum shared on his syndicated broadcast that Graham of his own initiative issued a statement clarifying publicly for the first time "his opposition to proselytizing the Jewish community, his commitment to American pluralism in which all religious and racial groups are full partners, and his conviction that Judaism . . . possesses a covenant from God which is 'eternal, forever,' and not subject to abrogation."[15]

In Graham's statement he affirmed: "Just as Judaism frowns upon proselytizing that is coercive, or that seeks to commit men against their will, so do I . . . along with most evangelical Christians, I believe God has always had a special relationship with the Jewish people . . . In light of that, I have never felt called to direct my evangelistic efforts to Jews or any other particular group."[16]

The religious revolution envisioned by the crafters of Key '73 fell far short of its goal. A dramatic rekindling of Christian faith across the United States was not realized. But what the effort did foster was dialogue and a deepened understanding between Jews and Christians.[17]

Graham's greatest positive impact on global Jewry was his support and defense of the Jewish State of Israel. His steadfast love of the Jewish State was not built upon an "end-time prediction" but a "now-time exhortation" and that "an end-time battle . . . will see Jews restored in greater security in their homeland."[18] His first visit in the 1960s included a lunch hosted by then Foreign Minister Golda Meir, which was followed by a press conference that Graham later said had been characterized as the largest press conference since Israel announced its independence. He would also meet with Israel's President, Yitzhak Ben-Zvi and hold three "evangelistic meetings," which attracted thousands of participants. They were configured as meetings because Prime Minister Ben Gurion opposed a large evangelical rally.[19]

Following the Six-Day War in June 1967, Graham maintained his steadfast and vocal support of Israel, urging its leaders not to yield to political pressure that would endanger Israel's security. He envisioned Jerusalem as an undivided Jewish city, called for evangelical-Jewish dialogue, and declared that "[t]he Jews are God's chosen people," and "We cannot place ourselves in opposition to Israel without detriment to ourselves."[20]

In the midst of the 1973 Yom Kippur War, Graham played a decisive role in helping Israel attain critical military aid. During the third and fourth days of the war, a stalemate developed between Secretary of State Henry Kissinger and Secretary of Defense James Schlesinger over whether the United States should send missiles to Israel through an emergency airlift. Prime Minister Golda Meir, unable to reach Nixon, called Graham during the night pleading for his intervention and expressing fears that within twenty-four hours, Israel could very well be defeated. According to Tanenbaum, Graham immediately called Nixon beseeching action, "God will judge you as to how you respond to Israel in its hour of need. That God forbid if anything should happen to Israel, you will have to bear the responsibility before the Lord, for failing the Jewish people in their hour of need."[21] The next morning, an impressive US military airlift would begin, one which US *Airforce Magazine* claimed was "justifiably called the airlift that saved Israel."[22]

Graham also mourned with the Jewish community. After the massacre at the 1972 Munich Summer Olympics in which Palestinian terrorists killed eleven Israeli athletes, Graham visited a San Francisco synagogue to join them in prayer at a memorial service.

Graham helped imperiled Jews in the Soviet Union, successfully advocating for and earning the release of several Soviet Jewish individuals who had been denied visas for great lengths of time. In 1971, his direct line to Kissinger helped secure the release from Potma Prison of Ruth Aleksandrovich, a twenty-three-year-old nurse who was on the verge of dying from arthritis and nephritis after imprisonment for the crime of purchasing a Bible on the black market. In 1972, he advocated through the Nixon administration for the successful release of Gavriel Shapiro, a Jewish activist, from prison. During a 1984 twelve-day tour in Russia, Graham visited Jewish synagogues in Moscow and Leningrad, meeting with Jewish leaders to discuss their aspirations and hardships. Afterwards, he spoke with Soviet officials about allowing more Jews to emigrate.[23]

Graham made consistent efforts to meet with Jewish communities behind the Iron Curtain. In September 1977, in the midst of a week-long crusade in Hungary, he met in a closed, off-the-record meeting with the Jewish religious and civic community and visited a synagogue gathering. He recalled weeping with them as they remembered the Nazi murder of 400,000 Hungarian Jews and reported that the 80,000 to 100,000 Hungarian Jews who survived were enjoying, for the first time in their history, the ability to freely enjoy Jewish education, culture, and worship.[24]

In 1978, Graham met with Jewish leaders of Poland and was deeply impacted by a visit to Auschwitz. In a statement issued from that death camp where one million Jews were murdered, he noted, "Auschwitz stands as a reminder for all humanity—as a reminder of one of the darkest periods in the whole history of civilization. It reminds us of the terrible potential man has for violence and inhumanity. We cannot claim the excuse of ignorance whenever we allow any portion of humanity to be scorned and harassed. Auschwitz also stands as a monument to the courage and the steadfastness of those who sought to fight the evil system that it represented. The Holocaust of Auschwitz, Birkenau, Dachau, Treblinka, and other camps reminds us of the courage and indestructibility of the Polish people and the Polish Jews and those from many other countries who died and suffered here." In a 1982 conversation with New England Jewish leaders he reflected: "I would like to think that the vast majority of people involved in that terrible hell, the Holocaust, were professing Christians and not real Christians."[25]

In 1985, when President Ronald Reagan had accepted the invitation of Germany's President Kohl to a ceremony of reconciliation at the Bitburg Cemetery not knowing that forty- nine members of the Waffen SS, a division of the elite Nazi guard who ran death camps, were buried there, Graham intervened. Graham spoke two times with Reagan and once with First Lady Nancy Reagan, reporting that he was "very strong with Reagan . . . I have never been so strong with him before—and told him that this was far more a moral issue than a political one, and that unless he finds a way to straighten this out it will undermine his moral authority in the country and overseas." Graham recounted that Nancy Reagan wished that Kohl would find a way to withdraw the invitation to the Bitburg cemetery and was angry with the staff who got them into this hole.[26] The itinerary would be amended. On May 5, 1985, Presidents Reagan and Kohl preceded their eight-minute visit to Bitburg's Kolmeshöhe Cemetery with a visit to Bergen-Belsen concentration camp where Reagan delivered a speech reported by *Time* magazine as a "skillful exercise in both the art of eulogy and political damage control."[27] Reagan remarked in his speech (which Rabbi Tanenbaum had a hand in helping to message): "All these children of God, under bleak and lifeless mounds, the plainness of which does not even hint at the unspeakable acts that created them. Here they lie. Never to hope. Never to pray, never to love. Never to heal. Never to laugh. Never to cry . . . And then, rising above all this cruelty—out of this tragic and nightmarish time, beyond the anguish, the pain and the suffering and for all time, we can and must pledge. Never again."[28]

Graham's steadfast stance of support earned him three awards from Jewish organizations: The Torch of Liberty Plaque by the Anti-Defamation League of B'nai B'rith in 1969, the International Brotherhood Award from the National Conference of Christians and Jews in 1971, and the American Jewish Committee's first National Interreligious Award in 1977.

In Graham's 1977 acceptance speech when he received the Interreligious Award from the AJC, he acknowledged that "the institutional church has sinned through much of its history and has much to answer for at the Judgment, especially for the anti-Semitism practiced against the Jewish people." He noted that just as Jews ask the question, "Who is a Jew," so must one ask, "Who is a Christian?" He opined that those who profess Christianity but fail to love their neighbor are not true Christians. And he outlined areas for future Jewish-evangelical partnership—working and praying for the peace of Jerusalem; working for better race relations in America (black and white, Jew and Gentile, majority and minorities); supporting our country that offers freedom and opportunity to Christians and Jews alike; creating common agreements for teaching moral law in public schools; working together for world peace, freedom, and justice; and working together for a national spiritual and moral awakening in America.[29]

Graham's influence over US presidents was immense—he had a relationship with every president from Truman to Obama. At a 1982 meeting with Jewish leaders from the New England region, Graham shared that while people thought he was close to Nixon, he saw President Johnson more than any other president, even preaching at his funeral. Graham then recalled a story that Johnson had told him. When President Kennedy was assassinated and Johnson set out for Washington, the first letter Johnson received was from his aunt who said, "Remember the Jews. Always be friends to the Jews and God will bless you. If you're not friends with the Jews, God won't bless you."[30]

That anecdote stayed with Graham, who made it part of his life's work to bless Israel and to bless the Jewish community through his preaching and through the work of his Billy Graham Evangelistic Association (BGEA) that had a global reach.

### Graham's Fall from Jewish Grace

After his retirement, Graham acknowledged with regret that there were times he crossed the lines between pastoring and politics. Critics maintained he was an apologist for Lyndon Johnson's Vietnam War and Nixon's Watergate scandal. *Time* magazine called Graham's relationship with Nixon, "his coziest—and costliest . . . Watergate not only left Graham personally disillusioned but also damaged his moral authority outside the evangelical world."[31]

While Watergate was a national nightmare and led to Nixon's humiliating resignation, the antisemitic comments made by Nixon inside the White House would become Graham's personal nightmare. Akin to Roosevelt and Truman, Nixon never made public antisemitic comments; however, as Brandeis University historian Steven Whitfield in the journal *Patterns of Prejudice* noted: "Inside the White House, Richard M. Nixon's remarks were often scurrilous. His antisemitism was not casual; it was close to compulsive. And it could be coupled with other seething grievances, for example, towards liberals, radicals, the media, Blacks and Italian-Americans."[32]

Graham, as pastor to the President, would become entangled in Nixon's string of antisemitic tirades, and his support of Nixon's antisemitic rants would seem to validate many Jewish fears unproven up until that time—that Graham's support of Jews was insincere, superficial, and that his foundational evangelical beliefs were antisemitic. The first glimpse of Graham's prejudicial attitudes, that predated the release of the secretly taped Oval Office recordings, came to light with the 1994 release of the diaries of Nixon's Chief of Staff H. R. Haldeman. Haldeman not only recalled Graham joining in with Nixon's discussion of the "total Jewish domination of the media" but also recalled Graham saying that the nation's problems lie with "satanic Jews."[33]

Upon hearing Haldeman's account, Graham professed to be in a state of disbelief and issued a public statement: "Those are not my words." He added: "I have never talked publicly or privately about the Jewish people, including conversations with President Nixon, except in the most positive terms."[34] This would prove to be untrue.

With the 2002 release of Nixon's secretly recorded tapes, Graham's voice of bigotry was undeniable. The call took place in the Oval Office on February 1, 1972. The President was complaining about Jewish control of the media. Graham, instead of challenging Nixon's prejudicial claims, added to them. To the statement, "I mean not all the Jews, but a lot of Jews are great friends of mine," he added a denigrating comment that undercut his public bond with American Jews: "They swarm around me and are friendly to me because they know that I'm friendly to Israel. But they don't know how I really feel about what they're doing to this country."[35]

In 2009, a second incriminating tape was circulated. It was a recording of a twenty-minute phone call from Graham to Nixon on February 21, 1973, just hours after Nixon addressed the country from the Oval Office about the Watergate scandal.

On this publicly released tape recording, Graham complained to Nixon about the Jewish opposition to Key '73 (in which all the major U.S. denominations of Christianity were joining together in an evangelistic effort for the first time), saying that Jews were going "right after the church." He shared with Nixon the upcoming meeting he had planned with Rabbi Tanenbaum for later that month. The President told Graham to be "very, very tough with all of our Jewish friends and Marc Tanenbaum. You tell him he's making a terrible mistake and they are going to get the darnedest wave of anti-Semitism here if they do not behave . . . This anti-Semitism is stronger than we think. It's unfortunate but this has happened to the Jews. It happened in Spain. It happened in Germany. Now it's going to happen in America if these people don't start behaving."[36]

Graham verbally agreed with Nixon saying, "The Bible talks about two kinds of Jews. One is called the synagogue of Satan. They're the ones putting out the pornographic literature. They're the ones putting out these obscene films."[37]

Nixon concluded the conversation saying, "It may be they have a death wish. You know that's been the problem with our Jewish friends for centuries."

The condemnation by many in the Jewish community was immediate and lasted from 2002 until after Graham's death. "Here we have an American icon, the closest we have to a spiritual leader of America, who has been playing a charade for all these years," Abraham H. Foxman, the national director of the Anti-Defamation League, said in an interview immediately following the release of the tapes. "What's frightening is that he has been so close to so many presidents, and who knows what else he has been saying privately."[38]

Though Foxman would later accept an apology by Graham, at the moment of the tape's release, he called for Graham to return the 1971 award from the National Conference of Christians and Jews. Washington journalist James D. Besser said that the remarks "should awaken Jews to the intense dislike for them among many evangelical Christians, except insofar as Jews are useful to the fulfillment of Christian apocalyptic prophecies."[39]

Rabbi Tanenbaum's widow, Dr. Georgette Bennett, recalled that even more disturbing than the condemnation was the silence. "Having known everything Billy Graham did for the Jewish community, I was appalled that no one was stepping forward to defend him." In an effort to keep alive her late husband's legacy of friendship and partnership with Graham, Dr. Bennett's 2002 letter to the *New York Times* called for forgiveness. "Evangelical Christianity is based on the premise that even the greatest sinner can be redeemed." She later noted that this letter was the sole defense of Graham from the Jewish community at the time.[40]

After his death in 2018, while a handful of Jewish voices stood in support of Graham, a preponderance of headlines and comments related to Graham's relationship with the Jewish people noted his lowest moment, leading most Jews to write off Graham's legacy. Typical of this canceling was a piece entitled "Billy Graham Proved That One Can Support Israel and Still Be an anti-Semite" in which longtime political analyst Bob Schneider wrote, "Billy Graham was an anti-Semite. He bought off on Henry Ford and Adolf Hitler's views that Jews control the media."[41]

In a rare tribute after Graham's death, Jonathan Tobin, Editor-in-Chief of the *Jewish News Syndicate*, expressed greatest sorrow not for the death of this ninety-nine-year-old great American evangelical leader but for the fact that most Jews dismissed this valued friend "as the epitome of '[holy] roller' who hated Jews." Tobin called upon the Jewish community to overcome "prejudices of the past" in order to respond to the "needs and realities of the present."[42]

## Graham's Contrition

In 2002, immediately following the release of the first tapes, the eighty-three-year-old Graham issued a four-sentence apology that many Jewish leaders felt was grossly inadequate. Graham never acknowledged uttering the statements; he said he had no recollection of it. Two weeks later, a more substantive apology was issued by his organization in which Graham stated: "I don't ever recall having those feelings about any group, especially the Jews, and I certainly do not have them now." Perhaps trying to protect his own reputation and his legacy, perhaps contrite and trying to help us reexamine his words in the context of his entire life, he continued: "My remarks did not reflect my love for the Jewish people. I humbly ask the Jewish community to reflect on my actions on behalf of Jews over the years that contradict my words in the Oval Office that day."[43]

Graham's final meeting with Jewish leaders was initiated not by Jewish leadership but of his own accord. In the midst of one of his final crusades in Cincinnati in 2002, he requested a private meeting with a group of Cincinnati's Jewish leaders: Neil Bortz, President of the Jewish Federation; Rick Marshall, Director of the Cincinnati Outreach; George Barnard, President of the Cincinnati Board of Rabbis; and Michael Rapp, President of the Jewish Community Relations Council of the Federation of Cincinnati. Battling Parkinson's disease, hearing loss, and other health problems, the humbled and apologetic Graham expressed genuine remorse. When Graham entered the room, the Rabbis stood in deference to him and he responded that it is he who should be on his knees. He acknowledged that his remarks from thirty years ago were unforgivable but he was nonetheless begging for forgiveness. The Jewish leaders accepted his apology.[44]

There was no response by Graham after the 2009 release of the tape recording of the February 21, 1973, call. It was likely that his Parkinson's had caused such a decline that his family shielded him from the news.[45]

Christian supporters sought to explain his taped remarks. Some proposed that Graham was speaking only of liberal Jews with whom he had political disagreements or of those Jews whom he viewed as unethical for distributing pornography. Regardless of whether Graham was speaking about a segment of the Jewish community and not its entirety, his words are offensive and dangerous. For a prominent evangelical minister to verbally assail Jews with the phrase "synagogue of Satan" could easily lead to violence against Jewish sanctuaries. That Graham's words were uttered in private and not meant for public consumption perhaps lessened the blow but still raised the issue of his genuine feelings towards Jews.

Leighton Ford, Presbyterian minister, evangelist, author, and Graham's brother-in-law (married to Graham's sister Jean) who worked with Graham for thirty years as associate evangelist and later as vice president of BGEA, shared that while Graham had outgrown his early fundamentalist influences, perhaps it was the remnants speaking in that room with Nixon. Ford said Graham was in awe of the leaders and presidents with whom he met. He was in the presence of power. "I think he was over his head in one sense and wanted to agree with Nixon," Ford commented, before continuing: "He should have challenged him but he didn't. How many of us would be willing to contradict him?"[46]

In the midst of the 1973 Nixon call, Graham was feeling pressured by the Jewish outcry against Key '73, was no doubt frustrated, and some of his early learned hostilities towards Jews emerged. Graham indeed failed, in the face of power, to muster the moral courage to call out Nixon's rage-filled rhetoric. But does his failure to refute antisemitic statements, his failure to muster moral courage in the Oval Office, warrant the full wrath of cancel culture?

## Weighing the Record of Graham's Life

Like the social media culture of the early 2020s, that is quick to cancel leaders and celebrities, alike, the Jewish community, carrying the weight of the historical trauma from the Holocaust and the German Christian soil from which it emerged, is justifiably suspicious. Like many Jewish leaders across the country, on February 18, 2018, I (in my role as a Charlotte rabbi, professor, and Jewish leader) received a call from Charlotte's local newspaper's religion editor, asking for a comment upon Graham's death, reflecting on Graham's relationship with the Jewish people. At the time, I declined to comment. I didn't have enough background on the topic to answer the inquiry. Now, several years later, as I find myself immersed in the Tanenbaum archives as part of my graduate studies and engaged in the work of social justice and interfaith leadership in Charlotte (a city of 960 churches where one exits the airport onto Billy Graham Parkway), I see the value in knowing Graham's more complete story.

All humans are imperfect, so all relationships are imperfect, and that of Graham with the Jewish community is no exception. The words he spoke privately to Nixon in 1972 and 1973 caused deep wounds when revealed to the public, but the solid foundations he built for evangelical-Jewish relationship remain salvageable. The Jewish community would be wise to reopen the pages recording the relationship and determine how to weigh Graham's use of his public voice of boundless influence to support the Jewish people, to affirm their place in God's covenant, and to denounce antisemitism against the hurtful, careless words he spoke to Nixon during two Oval Office encounters.

Graham's actions in support of American and worldwide Jewry really did speak louder than his two recorded antisemitic exchanges with Nixon. And perhaps it was his actions over decades and not his recorded words from the Oval Office that reflected his true spiritual wisdom and heart. For Jews seeking to build bridges today with their local evangelical communities, many of Graham's thoughtful words and actions can serve as a foundation for today's dialogue. But for such a dialogue to take place, we have to be willing to construct a balancing scale that allows for human imperfection rather than one that tips towards cancel culture.

## Acknowledgments

Special thanks to Dr. Gary Zola and Dr. Josh Garroway for their guidance, to the American Jewish Archives for making these archives available, and to Amy Lefkof and Elaine Rose Glickman for their editorial wisdom.

## Notes

1. On July 10, 2003, the National Archives released a 1947 diary penned by President Truman in the back pages of a real estate book. He stated, "The Jews, I find, are very, very selfish. They care not how many Estonians, Latvians, Finns, Poles, Yugoslavs or Greeks get murdered or mistreated as D[isplaced] P[ersons] as long as the Jews get special treatment. Yet when they have power, physical, financial or political neither Hitler nor Stalin has anything on them for cruelty or mistreatment to the underdog. Put an underdog on top and it makes no difference whether his name is Russian, Jewish, Negro, Management, Labor, Mormon, Baptist he goes haywire. I've found very, very few who remember their past condition when prosperity comes." The US Holocaust Memorial Museum director at the time of the diary's release noted that Truman's comments reflected "a sort of cultural anti-Semitism that was common at the time in all parts of American society." And yet, Truman's actions benefitting Jews spoke louder than the antisemitic words he had secretly penned. Monty Noam Penkower, professor emeritus of Jewish History at the Machon Lander Graduate School of Jewish Studies in Jerusalem, whose expertise is on the establishment of the State of Israel, notes that Truman's active rescue of Holocaust victims and refugees, Truman's ongoing support as US President of Jewish settlement in Palestine, and his being the first statesmen to recognize the State of Israel eleven minutes after its creation, qualifies him "as a great president." Monty Noam Penkower, "The Venting of Presidential Spleen: Harry S. Truman's Jewish Problem," *The Jewish Quarterly Review* 94, no. 4 (2004): 615–24.

2. Rafael Medoff, Holocaust historian, notes that while Jews electorally supported President Franklin Delano Roosevelt at the highest levels (85 percent–90 percent), Roosevelt's disparaging and

antisemitic comments are captured in transcripts and memos. First, at the 1943 Casablanca Conference, Roosevelt voiced support for denying the full restoration of rights for Jews living under the former Vichy regime in order to prevent Jewish domination in many professions as happened in Germany. Second, in a private memo recorded by Senator Burton Wheeler capturing a 1939 conversation between him and Roosevelt regarding the potential presidential candidacy of Secretary Cordell Hull, Roosevelt said that Hull's wife was partially Jewish, which would be a liability. Roosevelt said to Wheeler, "You and I know what kind of blood we have in our veins," referring to the alleged superiority of their Dutch blood in contrast to Jewish blood. Rafael Medoff, "The Jews Should Keep Quiet: Franklin D. Roosevelt, Rabbi Stephen S. Wise, and the Holocaust," *Jewish Broadcasting Service*, September 24, 2019, https://www.youtube.com/watch?v=kV0Esqn90RQ.

3. Grant Wacker, *One Soul at a Time: The Story of Billy Graham* (Grand Rapids: Wm. B. Eerdmans Publishing Co., 2019), xi.

4. In evangelical Christianity, one is not born Christian but one becomes one when he freely commits his life to Jesus. David Van Biema, "Billy Graham, the Father of Modern Christian Evangelism, Dies at 99," *Time Magazine*, February 21, 2018. Billy Graham, "The Evangelical Christian and the Jew in a Pluralistic Society," National Interreligious Award American Jewish Committee, October 28, 1977, in MS-603: The Rabbi Marc H. Tanenbaum Collection, 1945–1992; Series C: Interreligious Activities, 1952–1992, Box 21, Folder 6, Graham, Billy, 1977.

5. David Firestone, "Billy Graham Responds to Lingering Anger Over 1972 Remarks on Jews," *New York Times*, March 17, 2002.

6 Doctrinal Watchdog, "Billy Graham and Richard Nixon Discuss the Jews," YouTube video, August 11, 2019, https://www.youtube.com/watch?v=lumOWK0xS_A. Ironically, in its first century context, the references to "the synagogue of Satan" in the New Testament's Book of Revelation speak not to a building but to an assembly, and not to Jews but to gentiles fraudulently pretending to be pious Jews. Nonetheless, this phrase has been weaponized to justify hatred of Jews and fuel the fires of antisemitism. According to David Frankfurter, while interpreters have customarily assumed the "synagogue of Satan" (Rev. 2:9, 3:9) refers to Jews who ignored or denied Christ, it is John's declaration to "Gentile God-fearers claiming an affiliation with Judaism as a basis for Christ's salvation." Frankfurter suggests that "notwithstanding the phrase's anti-Semitic history as a condemnation of Judaism, John means 'synagogue of Satan' only as a rejection of those pretending to be Jews. The real Jews are the ones who, like John and his confederates, cleave to a strict, priestly interpretation of purity laws."

Amy-Jill Levine and Marc Zvi Brettler, *The Jewish Annotated New Testament* (New York: Oxford University Press, 2011), 469.

7. Adam Wambold, "Operation Nickel Grass: Turning Point of the Yom Kippur War," Richard Nixon Foundation, October 8, 2014.

8. As his daughter, Susie J. Tanenbaum shared in *Lilith* magazine, Rabbi Tanenbaum was a source of great pain for his family. Susie J. Tanenbaum, "Confronting My Father's Legacy," *Lilith*, April 16, 2021.

9. Arthur Gilbert, "Conversation with Billy Graham," *ADL Bulletin*, December 1967, 1.

10. Religious News Service, "Billy Graham to Jews and Christians: 'Let us Strengthen one another,'" October 31, 1977. Tanenbaum Collection, Series C, Box 21, Folder 6.

11. Press Release, "Billy Graham Confers with Jewish Leaders," *Religion News Service*, June 23, 1969. Tanenbaum Collection, Box 21, Folder 1.

12. Arthur Gilbert, "Conversation with Billy Graham," *ADL Bulletin*, 2.

13. Leonard Yaseen, *The Jesus Connection: To Triumph Over Anti-Semitism* (New York: Crossroad Publishing, 1985), ix.

14. Edward Fiske, "A 'Religious Woodstock' Draws 75,000," *The New York Times*, June 16, 1972.

15. "Billy Graham and Judaism," WINS Religion Commentary, Rabbi Marc H. Tanenbaum of the American Jewish Committee, March 4, 1973. Tanenbaum Collection, Box 21, Folder 4.

16. "Press Release by Billy Graham," March 1973, Tanenbaum Collection, Box 22, Folder 7.

17. Edward Trandahl, "Two Leaders Agree: Dream of Key 73 Unrealized," *Omaha World Herald*, January 19, 1974, Box 21, Folder 5.

18. Gilbert, "Conversation with Billy Graham."

19. Tanenbaum reported that there were about three hundred press people in attendance. Tanenbaum Collection, Series H: Media, CD-1042. Transcription Introduces Billy Graham; Graham speech, circa 1982. Bader Mansour, "When Billy Graham Visited Israel," *Baptists in Israel*, February 21, 2018, http://www.baptist.org.il/news/post/173/When-Billy-Graham-Visited-Israel-%E2%80%93-Bader-Mansour.

20. Graham felt deeply connected to Jerusalem and Israel on a personal basis in addition to valuing its biblical and political significance. His oldest son had been to the Middle East twenty-seven times. His eldest daughter and her husband went to Hebrew University and lived in Jerusalem for a year. His eldest son-in-law's grandmother is buried in Jerusalem. Graham, "The Evangelical Christian and the Jew in a Pluralistic Society." Gilbert,

"Conversation with Billy Graham." The 1970s release of the film "His Land" by Billy Graham's film studio popularized Christian theological support for Israel and marked the beginning of a liberal Jewish and evangelical Christian pro-Israel lobby. That support by the broader evangelical community was rooted in a theological understanding that Israel's regathering presaged the second coming of Jesus and the end of history. Daniel G. Hummel, "His Land and the Origins of the Jewish-Evangelical Israel Lobby," *Church History* 87, no. 4 (December 2018): 1119–51.

21. Tanenbaum discusses Billy Graham with Q & A, circa 1981. Tanenbaum Collection, Series H: Media, CD-1041.

22. The airlift took place from October 14 to November 14, 1973 (even though the ceasefire occurred on October 24) during which American aircraft flew approximately 570 missions and transported 22,395 tons of material to Israel. Adam Wambold, "Operation Nickel Grass: Turning Point of the Yom Kippur War." Walter J. Boyne, "Nickel Grass," *Air Force Magazine*, December 1998.

23. In 1970, his intervention with friends in Washington helped release Ruth Aleksandrovich, who was imprisoned by Soviet authorities in a Siberian labor camp. Correspondence from Tanenbaum to Graham, November 12, 1971, Tanenbaum Collection, Box 21, Folder 2. "Marc H. Tanenbaum book proposal, chapter drafts & notes for Billy Graham, *Graham, Billy—The Jews and Israel, 1984–1985*," Box 22, Folder 9. Correspondence from Tanenbaum to Graham, July 5, 1972, Box 21, Folder 3. "Dr. Billy Graham New York Press Conference, Tuesday, September 25, 1984," Box 21, Folder 9.

24. "Dr. Billy Graham Meeting with Hungarian Jewish Leaders," Tanenbaum Memo to AJC Area Directors, September 15, 1977, Box 21, Folder 6.

25. Transcript of statement by Dr. Billy Graham on his visit to Auschwitz, Thursday, October 12, 1978. Tanenbaum Collection, Box 21, Folder 7. Transcription Introduces Billy Graham; Graham speech, circa 1982, CD-1042.

26. "Billy Graham's Telephone Call with President Reagan," Confidential memo from Marc Tanenbaum to Howard Friedman, David Gordis and Leo Nevas, April 19, 1985, Box 22, Folder 1.

27. William R. Doerner, "Paying Homage to History," *Time Magazine*, June 24, 2001, accessed January 2, 2021, http://content.time.com/time/magazine/article/0,9171,141740,00.html.

28. "Reagan Masterpiece: 1985 Bergen-Belsen Speech," *WSJ Video*, May 5, 1985, accessed January 2, 2021, https://www.wsj.com/video/reagan-masterpiece-1985-bergen-belsen-speech/2E64EDA1-1704-4A1E-AFDF-419587348A68.html.

29. Graham, "The Evangelical Christian and the Jew in a Pluralistic Society."

30. Tanenbaum Collection, CD-1042. Transcription Introduces Billy Graham; Graham speech, circa 1982.

31. Sarah Pulliam Bailey, "Q & A: Billy Graham on Aging, Regrets, and Evangelicals," *Christianity Today*, January 21, 2011. "Mellowed Billy Graham Has World View," *Daily Herald* (Arlington Heights), August 31, 1981, Tanenbaum Collection, Box 21, Folder 8. David Van Biema, "Billy Graham, the Father of Modern Christian Evangelism, Dies at 99," *Time Magazine*.

32. Stephen J. Whitfield, "Nixon and the Jews," *Patterns of Prejudice* 44, no. 5 (2010): 432.

33. Firestone, "Billy Graham Responds."

34. Firestone, "Billy Graham Responds."

35. Firestone, "Billy Graham Responds."

36. Eric Fingerhut, "Nixon: If only the Jews would behave . . . ," *Jewish Telegraphic Agency*, June 24, 2009. Doctrinal Watchdog, "Billy Graham & Richard Nixon discuss the Jews."

37. Firestone, "Billy Graham Responds."

38. Firestone, "Billy Graham Responds."

39. Firestone, "Billy Graham Responds."

40. Georgette Bennett, telephone by author, April 11, 2021. Georgette Bennett, "Billy Graham, Then and Now," Letter to the Editor, *The New York Times*, March 19, 2002. Georgette Bennett, e-mail message to author, March 12, 2021.

41. Bob Schneider, "Billy Graham Proved That One Can Support Israel and Still Be an anti-Semite." *ChicagoNow*, February 21, 2018, https://www.chicagonow.com/politics-now/2018/02/billy-graham-proved-that-one-can-support-israel-and-still-be-an-anti-semite/. David Hollinger, "Billy Graham's Missed Opportunities," *New York Times*, February 21, 2018.

42. Jonathan Tobin, "What We Thought of the Rev. Billy Graham," *Jewish News Syndicate*, February 22, 2018, https://www.jns.org/opinion/what-we-thought-of-the-rev-billy-graham/.

43. Firestone, "Billy Graham Responds."

44. Latonya Taylor, "Jewish Leaders Accept Apology," *Christianity Today*, August 5, 2002. Grant Wacker, *One Soul at a Time: The Story of Billy Graham*, 233.

45. Leighton Ford affirmed that family protectiveness was the likely reason. Leighton Ford, interview by author, Charlotte, North Carolina, October 15, 2020.

46. Leighton Ford Interview.

# On Accountability and *T'shuvah*: Two Talmudic Stories of Ostracism

*Rabbi Neil Hirsch*

In mining the Rabbinic tradition for models of accountability, *nidui* (also referred to as *shamta* in Aramaic) warrants consideration. *Nidui* is best understood as a temporary ostracism imposed by one party on another. Given recent public disclosures of misbehavior, gender harassment, and sexual assault, an analysis of *nidui* and the possibility of *t'shuvah* can set a path forward to maintain a community's integrity and sanctity.

The Rabbis created this halachic structure to address misbehavior in public, specifically rejecting private adjudication. They established community-wide norms for how to both hold someone accountable and enable his re-entry after fulfilling his sentence. Despite problematic teachings that enabled wrongdoing within a community, the practices around *nidui* support an ethic of protecting the vulnerable, believing those who bring wrongdoing public, and embracing the potential for restoration.

There are several stories in the Talmud that deal with *nidui*. Two, in particular, illuminate how *t'shuvah* operates within the parameters of ostracism. In one case, the wrongdoer[1] successfully makes *t'shuvah*; in the other, the wrongdoer never walks that path. In holding up these two cases next to one another, we may come to see how *nidui* operates in the Rabbinic tradition as a device that holds wrongdoers accountable, maintains integrity, establishes justice, and promotes sanctity for the community. By tracing *nidui* from the Mishnah through the Gemara, the *Mishneh Torah*, and later codes, we can see how the halachic tradition deploys *nidui*

RABBI NEIL HIRSCH (NY10) serves Hevreh of Southern Berkshire, in Great Barrington, Massachusetts. He is a current DHL candidate at HUC-JIR, researching a variety of voices on accountability, justice, *t'shuvah*, and forgiveness.

as a method for communal accountability and a doorway toward restoration.

## Defining *Nidui*

Some translate *nidui* as excommunication, banishment, or censure, but the translation must be qualified. In the Gemara, Rav argues that the term *shamta* comes from a contraction of *sham* and *meitah*, meaning "there is a death." Sh'muel argues the term is derived from *sh'mamah y'hiyeh*, meaning "he shall be desolate."[2] I prefer to translate *nidui* as "temporary ostracism," for reasons I will note below.

This temporary ostracism is a communal tool developed in the Rabbinic period;[3] an individual triggers it by engaging in one or more of twenty-four specific transgressions.[4] These sins include sexual violations, unethical business dealings, or the committing of a *chilul HaShem*. *Nidui* is first mentioned in *Mishnah Mo-eid Katan* 3:1–2 in the context of other restricted conditions: The Rabbis wonder about the rules for Chol HaMo-eid for those who would not have the opportunity to prepare for the holiday. The *m'nudeh* is mentioned, as is a person who just came back from a trip abroad, a former captive, a prisoner, a *nazir*, or a leper. Like the prisoner or leper, the *m'nudeh* was outside of the community, without the opportunity to prepare for the festival.

Maimonides and later codifiers go on to clarify *nidui* as a one-month sentence.[5] If the *m'nudeh* repents within thirty days, then the one who placed the ban upon him grants release.[6] The Rabbis also consider early release for the *m'nudeh* if he does what is asked of him prior to the thirtieth day of his sentence.[7] In the case of *nidui*, if the person does not repent and make reparations within those first thirty days, his ostracism is extended for a second month. Should the *m'nudeh* remain unrepentant, his ostracism transforms into *cherem* (excommunication).[8] While *cherem* is the more recognizable punishment, the codes envision it as an extension of *nidui*, as *Hilchot Nidui v'Cherem* deals much more with *nidui* than it does with *cherem*.

Interestingly, the Gemara and later codes do not legislate the behaviors of *t'shuvah* necessary for one to be released from ostracism, except that if there was a financial infraction, the offender needs to make the other party whole again. The codes mandate *t'shuvah* for a *m'nudeh*, yet the standards for someone's repentance as valid and complete are not explicitly defined in the halachic literature related to ostracism and excommunication. Perhaps one would then look to the halachic literature on *t'shuvah* for instruction. Still in this instance, the qualifications for release from ostracism remain unclear.

Ostracism is a better word than excommunication to describe *nidui* because the *m'nudeh* presumably still lives in the community. Even though the Gemara and Maimonides both assert that changing one's location is a path to full *t'shuvah*,[9] moving one's family, home, and business to another community for the sake of repentance appears impractical. When leaders ostracize or excommunicate someone, they also impact that person's family and other interests. The codes legislate as if the *m'nudeh* is still living in the community,[10] although the halachah also notes that a ban imposed in one city is to be honored in another community.[11]

Metaphorically and psychologically, *nidui* bears resemblance to the experience of exile, even though the exiled person remains within the community. *Nidui* is more like a temporary restraining order, limiting one's ability to take part in the life of the community.[12] During the period of *nidui*, halachah prohibits the *m'nudeh* from counting in a *zimun* or a minyan.[13] Others are instructed to carry out little business with him.[14] Outside of his wife and children, those in the community are not to come within a certain distance of him.

*Nidui* is related to oath making, but one that places obligation upon someone else.[15] One's declaration of *nidui* on someone else is valid and binding until the party who imposes the ban releases the *m'nudeh* from it.[16] A *beit din* can impose *nidui* on another, students can hold one another accountable through *nidui*, and an individual can even self-ostracize if he deems it necessary.[17]

To understand *nidui* is to see how power plays out within the community. For instance, a *beit din* can impose *nidui* on a community member without any due process. If a student declares *nidui* on a peer, their rabbis are not bound to the ban against that student, but other students are. If a rabbi declares a student a *m'nudeh*, then the obligations for the ostracism are upon all members of the community.[18] In this way, *nidui* is an expression of the Rabbinic caste system.

*Nidui* establishes a wrongdoer as a communal pariah, prompting consideration about how a community is to engage with that person during and after his ostracism. What considerations does a community need to make when applying *nidui*? The following aggadot help to give perspective surrounding the use of *nidui* and the role of *t'shuvah*.

## Case 1: The Repentant Butcher

In BT *Mo-eid Katan* 16a–17b, the Rabbis discuss cases involving *nidui*. They also outline the restrictions upon the *m'nudeh* (an ostracized individual) and upon the community toward the *m'nudeh*. In BT *Mo-eid Katan* 16a, the following story is told:

> There was a butcher who acted contemptuously toward Rav Tuvi bar Mattanah. Abaye and Rava were appointed to decide on this case, and they ostracized him. Eventually, the butcher appeased Rav Tuvi, the claimant.
>
> Abaye asked, "How shall this be handled? Should we release him since the ostracism has not been in place for thirty days? By not releasing him, the Rabbis would not be able to come and purchase meat."
>
> Abaye said to Rav Idi bar Avin, "Have you heard anything regarding this sort of matter?"
>
> He said to him, "Rabbi Tachalifa bar Avini said in the name of Sh'muel, 'a blast of the shofar signaled his restriction and a blast of the shofar releases him.'"
>
> Abaye said to him [rejecting the argument], "These words apply to monetary related ostracisms. But for an ostracism related to contemptuous behavior, we do not release him until the ostracism has been in force for thirty days."

In this story, Abaye is faced with two main considerations: first, he must decide about the sort of consequence the butcher must suffer for doing harm to Rav Tuvi. Then, he must also weigh the term of the sentence after the butcher has repented.

Abaye is clear about what should be done with the butcher: the latter wronged Rav Tuvi and thus must be declared a *m'nudeh*. The butcher accepts the ruling and the consequences, eventually doing *t'shuvah* within his thirty-day sentence. The Rabbis then ask Abaye: is one to be released early from *nidui* upon fulfilling the obligations required of him?

The nature of the Rabbinic caste system cannot be ignored. Here, the position within the community matters, and it problematizes Abaye's decision-making process. Given the power dynamic within which Abaye operates, it would have been terrifying to insult Rav Tuvi by releasing the wrongdoer early. Furthermore, the threat of offending the Rabbis suffices for Abaye to pause and think through his position, regardless of the Rabbis' reasoning.

Abaye is caught in a double bind. He must choose between maintaining the integrity of the halachah and allowing for nonlegal factors in his decision-making. Significantly, Abaye is not pressured by the inherent power of *t'shuvah*, that it should move the legal deciders to release the repentant from his ostracism. Abaye is responding to an asymmetrical application of communal power, one that pressures the halachah. The Rabbis want meat,[19] using their status to push for leniency toward the butcher. Yet the conditions do not appear to warrant such leniency. If this were a financial matter alone, Abaye could declare *n'ziphah* for the butcher and release him early. However, the butcher's wrongdoing was not exclusively a money dispute, and being lenient then would be precedential on several fronts. It would establish that one could be released early from *nidui* for wrongdoing other than financial misconduct. It would also set the norm for powerful people to lobby rabbis to adjust a halachic status of others to serve their interests. These situations would clearly pervert the intent of the halachah and upend *nidui*'s effectiveness as a tool for communal accountability.

Surely saying no to the Rabbis was not a simple matter. The butcher's ostracism affected the Rabbis. A third party's dispute of the sentence can be considered, but it should not override legal norms. For *nidui* to be an effective tool for accountability, Abaye must keep the butcher in *nidui* for the entirety of the thirty-day sentence.

## Case 2: The Unrepentant Rabbinical Student

In *Mo-eid Katan* 17a, we encounter another story about abusive behavior, suffering consequences, unrealized *t'shuvah*, the use of power, and the eventual protection of the community from predatory and sinful behavior. As the Gemara continues its discussion of *nidui*, the following story is told:

> [1] Once there was a young rabbinical student who had a hateful reputation.
>
> Rav Yehudah asked, "How shall we act in this matter? Should we ostracize him? The Rabbis need him, yet to not ostracize him would desecrate God's name."

*He said to Rabbah bar bar Channah, "Have you heard anything about this?"*

*He said to him, "Thus said Rabbi Yochanan, 'What is the meaning of that which is written,* For the lips of the priest safeguard knowledge, and they seek Torah from his mouth, for he is a messenger of the Eternal of Hosts?[20] *If the teacher resembles an angel of God, people may seek Torah from his mouth. If he does not resemble an angel of God, they may not seek Torah from his mouth.'"*

*Rav Yehudah ostracized the rabbinical student.*

*[2] Some time later, Rav Yehudah became ill. The Rabbis came to ask after him, and the ostracized rabbinical student came with them. When Rav Yehudah saw him, he laughed.*

*The rabbinical student said to Rav Yehudah, "Is it not enough that you have ostracized a person, but you also laugh at me?"*

*Rav Yehudah said to him, "I am not laughing at you; rather, when I go to the World to Come, my mind will be cheered knowing that I did not flatter someone even of your stature."*

*[3] Rav Yehudah died, and the rabbinical student came to the study hall saying, "Release me!"*

*The Rabbis said, "There is no one here of Rav Yehudah's stature who can release you. Rather, go to Rav Yehudah Nesiah, who can release you."*

*[4] The rabbinical student went to Rav Yehudah Nesiah. Rav Yehudah Nesiah said to Rav Ami, "Go and look into this case. If it is required to release him, then release him."*

*Rav Ami looked into the rabbinical student's claim, and thought to release him. However, Rav Sh'muel bar Nachmani rose to his feet and said, "Since the maidservant of the Rabbi's household,[21] the Sages did not treat ostracism lightly for three years, then for Rav Yehudah our colleague, all the more so should we take this case seriously."*

Rabbi Zeira said, "How do we explain what has happened before us, that today this elder, Rav Sh'muel, came to the study hall, where for many years he has not? *Learn from this that it is not necessary to release the rabbinical student."*

*Rav Yehudah Nesiah did not release the rabbinical student.*

*[5] The rabbinical student left. He was walking along, weeping. A wasp came, stung him on his penis, and he died.*

*They brought his body to the cave of the pious, but they did not accept it. They brought it to the cave of the judges, and they accepted it. What is the reason for this? Because he acted according to Rav Ilai, as was taught in a baraita:*

*Rav Ilai says, "If a person sees that his evil inclination is overpowering him, he should go to a place where they do not recognize him. He should dress in black and wrap himself in black, and he shall do what his heart desires. He should not desecrate the Heavenly Name publicly."*

This story can be broken into several sections, each display-
ing an insight into how the imposition of status affects both the
*m'nudeh* and the community. Just as with the butcher and Rav
Tuvi, the case of the rabbinical student and Rav Yehudah shows
that the Rabbis are concerned less with the specifics that would
lead to the declaration of *nidui* and more in maintaining the community's integrity.

In the first section, we meet an unnamed rabbinical student who
has a bad reputation. At the end of the story, the rabbinical student
dies from a wasp sting to his penis. To this point, the *Tosafot* note
that we can assume he earned his sinful reputation because of sexual wrongdoing.[22] Rav Yehudah considers the rumors about this
student and wonders, "Is it appropriate to temporarily ostracize
him?" This question is the cornerstone of the story.

Rav Yehudah asks because he is wrestling with a conflict similar to Abaye's thinking about granting the butcher early release.
Here, Rav Yehudah's consideration has at least two factors. First,
he considers the costs to the community of keeping the person in
his role. The Rabbis have a use for the rabbinical student to play
in the community. A ban would limit what he could do. However,
Rav Yehudah also notes the problem of someone of ill repute serving in one of those seats. Rav Yehudah takes the rumors seriously;
he does not discount them. The questions at hand are not legal,
Rabbah bar bar Channah reminds Rav Yehudah. They are a matter
of communal sanctity and integrity, like the sacred trust that the
biblical priests carried. People come to seek Torah from the rabbinical student, which is corrupted by his transgressions. Rabbis
and rabbinical students are nothing short of messengers of God.
For one of them to teach Torah while being a rumored wrongdoer
would be endorsing a *chilul HaShem*.

Like Abaye and Rava determining the butcher's status, Rav
Yehudah gives some consideration, although he does not hold a
full hearing, before declaring *nidui*. Significantly, he takes the rumors as valid evidence against the rabbinical student. As in the
first story, we see other priorities that motivate Rav Yehudah's
decision-making. Rav Yehudah at first is not fully confident in his
decision; some part of him does not want to ostracize the rabbinical student. "That is not desirable since the Rabbis need him," he
thinks. But Rav Yehudah values the sanctity of God's name over
the need to fill seats in communal roles.

No one comes forward with direct accusations against the rabbinical student; rather, the rumors serve as evidence for the judgment against him. One does not need to establish the factuality of the rumors to warrant the rabbinical student's ostracism. The nature or specifics of the rabbinical student's crimes matter little because the effect is enough, meaning that the perception of his bad reputation is sufficient to outweigh his utility to Rav Yehudah and the Rabbis and to warrant *nidui*. Moreover, the rabbinical student does not do what he needs to do to be released from *nidui*, namely make *t'shuvah*. When Rav Yehudah becomes ill, the rabbinical student goes to the rabbi's bedside, pleading, "Release me!" But Rav Yehudah laughs, saying that his decision to ostracize him was a good one. The rabbinical student exhibits no remorse, offers no apology; he only demands to be released from his ostracism.

The discomfort of being ostracized animates the rabbinical student's actions. Presumably, he knows how *nidui* works: the one who issued the ban is the one who has the ability to release him. That is why he shows up at Rav Yehudah's bedside. If Rav Yehudah dies, the most direct path out of *nidui* dies with him. The rabbinical student is fixated on Rav Yehudah's imminent demise and what that means for him, failing to grasp that he, too, holds a key to his own release. The rabbinical student fails to recognize the agency he has in his own release. Rav Yehudah's laughter at the rabbinical student is telling. He is saying to the rabbinical student, "You don't get it! You need to do *t'shuvah*. That you have shown up here making this demand proves that you continue to misunderstand."

Repentance could have paved the rabbinical student's path back to the community. In the opening chapter of his *Shaarei T'shuvah*, Rabbeinu Yonah of Gerona writes, "And know, that the sinner who delays his repentance, makes his situation ever graver day by day. He knows that God's wrath comes for him, and still he has a refuge to which he can turn. That refuge is *t'shuvah*."[23] The missing ingredient in this story is what the halachic texts provide: If someone returns in *t'shuvah* during his ostracism, release is permissible. The wrongdoer suffers the consequences of ostracism first, then *t'shuvah* gives the possibility for restoration. The rabbinical student never takes up that essential task.

The legal problem of this case lies in sections 4 and 5, after Rav Yehudah's death. Only someone of equal stature to Rav Yehudah has the power to release the *m'nudeh* from his ostracism. The rabbinical student never did *t'shuvah*, and Rav Yehudah affirmed his decision before dying.

The rabbinical student brings his case to Rav Yehudah Nesiah, in hopes of being released. Like the case of the butcher, Rav Yehudah Nesiah calls upon others to investigate the matter. Rav Ami does and ultimately argues for the rabbinical student's release, although we are not privy to Rav Ami's reasoning. Instead, Rav Sh'muel bar Nachmani rises to his feet, citing a separate precedent, calling for the rabbinical student to be treated in a similar fashion as the *m'nudeh* in that other instance. This unrepentant *m'nudeh* should be treated the same as any other unrepentant *m'nudeh*.

After Rav Sh'muel makes his case, another rabbi makes an assertion solidifying the rabbinical student's status as a *m'nudeh*. "Rabbi Zeira says: 'What has happened before us that, just today, this elder, Rav Sh'muel bar Nachamni, came to the study hall, whereas for many years he has not come?'" Rashi comments that Rav Sh'muel's presence is providential. Rav Sh'muel did not know that this case would come up at this moment and thinks it unwise to counter a precedent set in a prior case. Based on Rav Sh'muel's concern for the integrity of the established halachah and the fortune of his being present that day, Rav Yehudah Nesiah does not release the rabbinical student from *nidui*.

## A Troubling Element

Section 5 is the most dramatic. As the rabbinical student walks away from the study hall, dejected, a wasp stings him on his penis, and he dies, evidencing his wrongdoing as sexual. The authorities do not accept him at the Cave of the Pious. However, they do at the Cave of the Judges, using a troubling *baraita* as justification: "If a person sees that his evil inclination is overwhelming him, he should go to a place where they do not recognize him and clothe himself in black and wrap himself in black, and he should do what his heart desires. And he should not desecrate the Heavenly Name openly." Some people are compelled by the *yetzer hara*. Those who cannot overcome their urges should find a covert location to enable their behaviors without publicly committing a *chilul HaShem*.

The *baraita* with which the story concludes is the most damning element, as it sanctions sin and harm against others. Rav Ilai suggests that such behavior is not acceptable in one's own community, but would be permissible when disguised. This recognizes a tendency that must be overcome: the instinct for self-preservation by covering up one's wrongdoings. If he needs to do what would otherwise be considered sinful, he should go somewhere others will not recognize him. This *baraita* condones sin, enables harm, and abandons victims.

Given what we know about gender harassment, sexual assault, abuse, and trauma today, Rav Ilai's assertion runs counter to an ethic that protects the vulnerable. In truth, by sanctioning the performance of transgressions in secret, Rav Ilai enables and perpetuates harm.[24] In his commentary on this *baraita*, Rashi quotes a teaching of Rav Hai Gaon, noting that, surely, the Rabbis were not legislating a method by which one could sin. Rather, one wears black to conquer his heart, pushing himself away from the temptations of his evil inclination. That Rashi questions this teaching, even while apologizing for it, highlights the outrageousness of Rav Ilai's teaching.

Rav Yehudah has a conflict: reinstating the rabbinical student, regardless of the rationale, enables wrongdoing, which threatens the community. Condoning a sinner undermines the community, perpetuating violence. Writing about contemporary cases of abuse in Jewish institutions, lawyer and social worker Shira Berkovits writes, "Given that so few victims disclose abuse, institutions have a moral responsibility when faced with knowledge of abuse to communicate with their constituents . . . Moreover, when institutions have knowledge of abuse, they must communicate with other institutions where that individual works."[25]

The condoning of one transgression promotes the acceptance of other misdeeds and the corruption of a communal ethic. If the rabbinical student with the hateful reputation is not held publicly accountable, it undermines the community's integrity and sanctity.


### An Alternate Reading

Taken at face value, this *baraita* undoes all that comes before it. However, if one reads the sections of the story in a different order, new meaning emerges. Rav Ilai offers a path for sinners to sin, which cannot stand. Readers witness the considered approach that Rav Yehudah takes to this case, his dedication to halachah and the sanctity of the Rabbinate. In the end, he chooses communal integrity by using *nidui* for a rumored wrongdoer. Read in this way, Rav Yehudah's laughter is a rebuke of Rav Ilai. He does not legislate acceptance of the rabbinical student's *yetzer hara*. Instead, he accepts the rumors as valid. As Rabbi Mira Wasserman has written about this episode: "Rav Yehuda recognized that rumors are an important measure of communal health and flourishing. The institution of the rabbinic ban effectively moved misbehavior from the shadowy realm of secrets and rumors into the light of public attention. Most of the time, the threat of public shaming was enough to deter abuses of power. But when there was reason to suspect that abuse was happening, rabbis did not hesitate to make their accusations public."[26] Rav Yehudah brings the rumors to light, enabling the community to live by a particular ethic, and thus he maintains its sanctity and integrity.

Placing the rabbinical student in *nidui* confined him, preventing further harm. While the rabbinical student's experience was one of ostracism and constriction, such a ban was also a release for the community from the oppression of an abuser. Ostracizing a wrongdoer impacts both the direct parties involved and the community more broadly. The communal value of holding a wrongdoer accountable for his misdeeds matters.

## Conclusion

*Nidui* speaks to the enduring value of accountability for the sake of justice; holding someone accountable addresses an injustice. And, unlike excommunication or exile, the fact that *nidui* is temporary sparks a conversation about a *t'shuvah* process for both those who have experienced harm and those who have done wrong. *Nidui* stands out not only as a model for accountability, but as we learn from both Abaye and Rav Yehudah's reasonings, a way to promote communal integrity and sanctity. Then, as today, bringing accusations public allowed the Rabbis to operate outside of shadows, establishing credibility for the institutions they served. Recent public cases of gender harassment and sexual assault prompt examination of our institutions' systems for accountability and raise questions about the role of *t'shuvah*. As a Jewish community, our textual tradition has a voice in current conversations. Seeing the attention that Abaye and Rav Yehudah give to all parties involved in the cases they considered is illustrative for our time as well.

## Notes

1. I prefer the English term "wrongdoer" to refer to the person who is ostracized. Some may describe him as an offender, transgressor, perpetrator, or sinner. Describing the individual as a wrongdoer allows him to have committed a range of misdeeds, without passing judgment on the magnitude of his crime. For ease, I also refer to the wrongdoer consistently with male pronouns, because in the two cases explored here both wrongdoers are men.

2. BT *Mo-eid Katan* 17a.

3. Most of the Talmudic conversation on *nidui* is found in BT *Mo-eid Katan* and BT *N'darim*, though references are found in several tractates. The medieval codes are comprehensive in their collection of the various halachot regarding *nidui*, giving readers a unified corpus to examine.

4. BT *B'rachot*, 19a; *Mishneh Torah, Hilchot Talmud Torah* 6:14; *Shulchan Aruch, Yoreh Dei-ah* 334:43.

5. *Mishneh Torah, Hilchot Talmud Torah* 7:6; *Yoreh Dei-ah* 334:1.

6. *Mishneh Torah, Hilchot Talmud Torah* 7:3; *Yoreh Dei-ah* 334.

7. The Rabbis also consider a related status known as *n'ziphah*, a seven-day censure, which was reserved for limited financial transgressions that were easily remedied. *Mishneh Torah, Hilchot Talmud Torah* 6:14; *Yoreh Dei-ah* 334:14.

8. *Mishneh Torah, Hilchot Talmud Torah* 6:14; *Yoreh Dei-ah* 334:14.

9. BT *Rosh HaShanah* 16b; *Mishneh Torah, Hilchot T'shuvah* 2:4.

10. *Mishneh Torah, Hilchot Talmud Torah* 7:4; *Yoreh Dei-ah* 334:2.

11. *Mishneh Torah, Hilchot Talmud Torah,* 6:13; *Yoreh Dei-ah* 334:20.

12. *Mishneh Torah, Hilchot Talmud Torah* 7:4; *Yoreh Dei-ah* 334:2.

13. *Mishneh Torah, Hilchot Talmud Torah* 7:4; *Yoreh Dei-ah* 334:2.

14. *Mishneh Torah, Hilchot Talmud Torah* 7:4; *Yoreh Dei-ah* 334:2.

15. BT *N'darim* 7a.

16. *Mishneh Torah, Hilchot Talmud Torah* 7:2–3; *Yoreh Dei-ah* 334:15–16.

17. *Mishneh Torah, Hilchot Talmud Torah* 7:9–14; *Yoreh Dei-ah* 334:15–16.

18. *Mishneh Torah, Hilchot Talmud Torah* 6:13; *Yoreh Dei-ah* 334:15–16.

19. Ritva (Rabbi Yom Tov ibn Ashvili, fourteenth-century Spain) on *Mo-eid Katan* 16a.

20. Mal. 2:7.

21. BT *Mo-eid Katan* 17a. A maidservant sees a man striking his oldest son. She declares that the man should be in *nidui*, and his ban is upheld for three years. Presumably the man remained unrepentant like the rabbinical student.

22. *Tosafot* on *Mo-eid Katan* 17a. The narrative hides the rabbinical student's victims from the readers. They are almost anonymous in their pain. This may advantage a contemporary reading in that the legal deciders hearing the case presume the rumors are true. Still, by not expressing any halachic or human concern for the harm the rabbinical student inflicted on others, this text silences and devalues victims.

23. *Shaarei T'shuvah* 1:2.

24. For a contemporary analogue, see Amos N. Guiora, *Armies of Enablers: Survivor Stories of Complicity and Betrayal in Sexual Assaults* (Chicago: American Bar Association, 2020). Reflecting on the experience of victims of sexual assault on college campuses, legal scholar Guiora argues, "Without the enablers, the perpetrators would not have had the enormous confidence and impunity to act as they did." Through this lens, we might say that Rav Ilai's teaching would enable wrongdoing.

25. Shira M. Berkovits, "Institutional Abuse in the Jewish Community," *Tradition* 50, no. 2 (2017): 42.

26. Mira Wasserman, "The Torah on #MeToo, Slander, and Naming Perpetrators," *The Forward*, March 27, 2018.

# The Gender Wage Gap in the Reform Movement: An Updated United Data Narrative

*Savannah Noray*

### Preface

The following article by Savannah Noray serves as an update to the work of the Reform Pay Equity Initiative (RPEI). This report builds on the information found in the Fall 2018 *CCAR Journal: The Reform Jewish Quarterly* symposium "Pay Equity Within the Reform Movement" and provides an update to Dr. Elyse Gould's symposium article "The Gender Wage Gap in the Reform Movement: A United Data Narrative," which documented the first aggregation of data concerning the gender-based wage gap in the Reform Movement.[1]

In its sixth year, the RPEI is a consolidated effort of the seventeen organizations of the Reform Movement to educate employees and employers about the wage gap, to collect data, and to promote the use of interventions such as posting salary ranges, counterbalancing implicit bias, and offering paid family and medical leave. The work of the Reform Pay Equity Initiative can be found at www.reformpayequity.org.

The article below uses the data of the American Conference of Cantors (ACC), Association of Reform Jewish Educators (ARJE), Central Conference of American Rabbis (CCAR), Early Childhood Educators of Reform Judaism (ECE-RJ), and the National Association of Temple Administration (NATA). These are the five professional

SAVANNAH NORAY, MSc Applied Economics, is a Public Policy PhD student at Harvard University specializing in labor economics. Her research aims to understand the constraints that women face when pursuing their careers and how institutions can minimize these barriers.

organizations within the Reform Movement currently tracking employment data. However, the work of the RPEI involves all the organizations within our Movement, deepening the efforts within the individual organizations for their employees and constituents and creating synergy among the groups to affect change broadly.

— Rabbi Marla J. Feldman and Rabbi Mary L. Zamore,
Co-Leaders, Reform Pay Equity Initiative

## Introduction

In 2020, the average woman earned 84 percent of what the average man earned in the United States.[2] Many factors contribute to this wage gap. For example, men may be more likely to study STEM subjects in college, thus setting them up for higher paying jobs than women.[3] At the same time, negative and inaccurate stereotypes about women's abilities could also contribute to the wage gap.[4] In addition, women may be reluctant to request pay raises, which could further mute their earnings.[5] Moreover, women may be more likely to work in occupations that give them the flexibility to manage childcare, and these occupations may compensate for providing this amenity by offering lower salaries.[6] In short, the gender wage gap is a complex issue with many potential determinants. Thus, measuring the success of initiatives aimed at reducing the gap is crucial to ensuring effective policy design.

An important first step towards evaluating whether polices have succeeded at closing the gap is comparing outcomes before and after the policies have been implemented. Towards that end, this report analyzes the current state of the gender gap across various professions in the Reform Movement and, when possible, documents how the gap has changed since the ongoing interventions proposed by the Reform Pay Equity Initiative (RPEI) began.[7] The data that provide the point of comparison were summarized in a report using similar data from 2016–2017.[8] For ease of comparison, the figures and statistics presented in this report closely mirror those contained in Gould (2018) whenever possible.

There are two main dimensions along which this report analyzes pay equity. First, this report analyzes how men and women sort into various occupations within the Reform Movement. From this analysis, we can learn whether men and women tend to take jobs with systematically different pay, thus potentially leading to a greater overall pay gap between men and women. Studying gender segregation is related to pay equity insofar as it leads to aggregate pay disparities or reflects barriers to female Jewish professionals' career choices. Second, this report studies pay equity more directly by analyzing differences in pay *within* occupations. This analysis holds constant broad job characteristics, such as the tasks typically performed or educational requirements. Therefore, pay disparities within occupations reflect a slightly narrower set of potential causes, such as job experience, type of congregation/school served, and geographic location. Finally, this report briefly summarizes the state of paid leave, a workplace amenity that often disproportionately affects women's work choices.

Comparing the data between 2016–2017 and 2019–2020, rabbis showed the most progress towards pay equity while cantorial and temple administrator positions demonstrated no progress. Two of three categories of rabbinical positions showed progress towards more equitable pay. In contrast, the pay gap among cantors and temple administrators stayed roughly the same. Breaking down by congregation size, senior/solo rabbi pay became more equitable across two out of three congregation size categories (and stayed constant otherwise). In contrast, the gender pay gap among individuals in cantorial positions has remained roughly the same (or even grown slightly) across all three congregation sizes. This main finding and other results that provide important context are summarized below. The body of the report expands on each of these points in greater detail:

- Women tend to be found in education-related occupations. Of the data analyzed, the occupation category with the lowest fraction of women is full-time congregational rabbis, where 38 percent of senior/solo, associate, and assistant rabbis are women.
  - Female representation among senior/solo rabbis decreases as congregation size increases.
  - While these overall trends are consistent with earlier findings in Gould (2018), a meaningful increase in female representation has occurred across all categories. For example, while only 25 percent of senior/solo rabbis were women in 2016–2017, this fraction rose to 30 percent in 2020.

- Women report lower base salaries than men across the occupations covered in the data. Gaps in education-related occupations are relatively low (female educators earn 6 percent less than their male counterparts), while the gap rises to 8–18 percent across some rabbinical, cantorial, and temple administrator positions.
  - The pay gap for senior/solo rabbis narrows as congregation size increases. In contrast, the pay gap for cantors widens as congregation size increases.
  - Again, the general trends mirror those reported in Gould (2018). Comparing pay gaps over time, there is reason for both optimism and pessimism. Pay gaps decreased among senior/solo rabbis and assistant rabbis, while increasing among associate rabbis. The decreased pay gap among senior/solo rabbis was concentrated among the smallest congregations (300 or fewer members) and largest congregations (600 or more members), while midsized congregations (301–599 members) saw no change. In contrast, among cantors, the pay gap slightly increased or stayed the same across all congregation size categories.
- Individuals in cantorial positions receive generous paid parental leave, while rabbinical, education-related, and administrative occupations in the Reform Movement offer comparatively less leave.
- The data available for this report are a significant improvement over what was available for the analysis in Gould (2018). That said, data collection methods, data quality, and methodological limitations still make drawing conclusions difficult. To understand what is driving the gap and what solutions are helping to close it, improving data further would be valuable.

## Data Sources and Limitations

This report pulls from multiple sources of data, as outlined in Table 1. Broadly speaking, the data sources cover rabbis, cantors, educators, and temple administration professionals across the Reform Movement. Each data source is associated with a specific member organization of the Reform Pay Equity Initiative (RPEI), which is co-led by Women of Reform Judaism (WRJ) and the Women's Rabbinic Network (WRN). The American Conference of Cantors

| Data Source | Year | Data Collection | Respondent Occupations | # Respondents | # Female Respondents | # Male Respondents |
|---|---|---|---|---|---|---|
| Salary Survey for the American Conference of Cantors (ACC) | 2019 | Online questionnaire sent via email | • Senior/Solo Cantor • Assistant Cantor • Sole Spiritual Leader • Retiree • Cantor/Educator • Cantor/Rabbi | 209 | 141 (67.4%) | 66 (31.5%) |
| Compensation and Benefits Survey for National Association for Temple Administration (NATA) | 2019 | Online questionnaire sent via email | • Executive Director • Temple Administrator | 217 | 144 (66.4%) | 73 (33.6%) |
| Compensation Study for Central Conference of American Rabbis (CCAR) | 2019-2020 | Administrative data | • Senior/Solo Rabbi • Associate Rabbi • Assistant Rabbi • Rabbi Educator | 671 | 269 (40%) | 402 (60%) |
| Association of Reform Jewish Educators (ARJE) | 2020 | Online questionnaire sent via email | • Director of Education • Religious School Principal • Assistant Director (Synagogue/Religious School setting) • Teacher/Professor • Camp Professional • Youth Professional • School Administrator • Rabbi/Cantor | 247 | 197 (78.2%) | 49 (19.4%) |
| Compensation and Benefits Survey for Early Childhood Educators of Reform Judaism (ECE-RJ) | 2019 | Online questionnaire sent via email to directors, then directors shared survey with other faculty at the school | • Teacher • Assistant teacher • Directors of Early Childhood Education • Preschool Director • Assistant Director • Director of Lifelong Learning | 502 (125 unique schools) | 490 (97.6%) | 12 (2.4%) |

Table 1: Data Sources

*Notes:* The total number of respondents is sometimes higher than the sum of female and male respondents because some respondents chose not to disclose their gender.

(ACC) data includes information on the salaries, benefits, and personal characteristics (e.g., work experience) of members. Similar information is collected from various types of educators in the data sets sourced through the Association of Reform Jewish Educators (ARJE) and the Early Childhood Educators of Reform Judaism (ECE-RJ). These data sets are female dominated (as are the professions themselves), so the pay inequality analysis using these data is somewhat limited. Data from the National Association for Temple Administration (NATA) covers executive directors and temple administrators. Finally, data from the Central Conference of American Rabbis (CCAR) provides information on full-time rabbis who are members of the CCAR serving Union for Reform Judaism congregations and are actively contributing to the Reform Pension Plan during the 2019–2020 congregational year.

Before discussing the results, it is worth noting some limitations. One primary limitation is that all data sources except for the CCAR are collected through an online questionnaire sent to respondents via email. This poses several issues. First, this means that the data represent a sample of individuals who decided to reply to the survey.[9] This matters because people who did not reply to the survey may differ from respondents in meaningful ways, therefore resulting in a less representative sample of individuals—for example, perhaps nonrespondents work more and have higher salaries. A second concern is that respondents may misreport information. This could happen for a variety of reasons: the respondents are trying to complete the questionnaire quickly, they cannot remember an answer, or they simply make an entry error. A third concern is that the sample size is low for some of the data sources, which means that the statistics reported may lack precision. In contrast to these issues, the CCAR data are administrative and thus cover the universe of pension-participating rabbis while being less likely to contain misreporting errors.

In addition to data quality concerns, there is a methodological limitation that applies to all data sources. In order to make claims about what factors are *causing* certain trends, social scientists typically rely on data that track individuals over time during which a randomly selected subgroup are exposed to the causal factor of interest. For example, a formal test of whether the RPEI efforts lead to more pay equity would require that a random subset of individuals was exposed to RPEI programming ("treatment group") while others were not ("control group"). In this case, any outcomes that were different between these two groups over time would then be attributable to the programming efforts. While this report tracks outcomes over time, the lack of a control group precludes any causal inference. Therefore, this report focuses on building rich descriptive insights and refrains from making definitive causal claims.

A final cautionary note for interpreting these results is that while most of the data were collected prior to the COVID-19 pandemic, the ARJE collected data over a timeframe that overlapped with the pandemic. Therefore, an additional concern is that some of the results derived from the ARJE data are driven by the unique circumstances of the pandemic. In fact, a third of the respondents in the ARJE (33.3 percent) noted that their base salary was affected by COVID-19 in some way, usually in the form of a salary decrease or freeze. Relevant to this report, women were more likely to report being affected (35 percent versus 26 percent). Results from the ARJE thus ought to be interpreted with this in mind.

## Gender Differences in Occupational Sorting

One major reason why women earn less than men is because they tend to be in occupations that pay less (Goldin, 2014). This same pattern exists within the Reform Movement. Broadly speaking, women are less likely to be in lucrative occupations, and even within high paying occupations, women are less likely to be in the highest paying positions. Insofar as these patterns reflect barriers to career advancement or choice for women, this is a valuable metric to track.

Women in the Reform Movement are particularly likely to be in jobs related to education, which mimics a broader trend in the economy. While the ARJE and ECE-RJ data are not likely to be perfectly representative of the population of educators in their organizations, respondents were overwhelmingly female (78 percent and 98 percent, respectively), thus suggesting that the occupations surveyed are female-dominated as well. With the same caveats about representativeness in mind, cantors and temple administrators are more likely to be female: around 67 percent of cantor respondents and 66 percent of temple administrator respondents are women. In contrast, only 38 percent of full-time congregational rabbis[10] are women.

Similar patterns emerge when taking a closer look at rabbis. Figure 1 breaks out rabbis by position and congregation size across gender. The middle set of bars shows that senior/solo rabbi positions are dominated by men (70 percent male, 30 percent female). In contrast, assistant rabbis and associate rabbis are 47 percent and 64 percent female, respectively. Mimicking the broader pattern of female representation in education-related occupation categories,

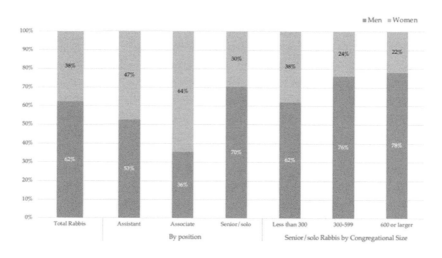

Figure 1: Gender-based sorting among rabbis

*Note:* Source is 2020 CCAR data.

rabbi educators are the most female-dominated position (74 percent female).

The set of bars on the right in Figure 1 focuses on senior/solo rabbis. As congregation size gets larger, the share of females in senior/solo rabbi positions tends to become smaller. While women make up 38 percent of senior/solo rabbis in the smallest-sized congregations, they make up only 22 percent of the rabbis among the largest congregations. Given that 30 percent of all senior/solo rabbis are female, it is clear that women are overrepresented in small congregations while underrepresented in large ones.

The gender-based sorting across occupation categories, rabbinical positions, and congregation size implies that more female entry into rabbinic occupations, higher paying positions (e.g., senior/solo rabbi), or larger congregations would result in a lower *overall* pay gap. Comparing this analysis to Gould (2018), sorting patterns seem to be trending towards more women in more lucrative positions. While 32 percent of full-time congregational rabbis were female in 2016–2017 (the time period analyzed in Gould [2018]), this fraction has increased to 38 percent over the course of two years—representing a relatively rapid rise of women in these leadership positions.[11] Specifically, this increase is due to a larger share of women in the higher paying positions of associate and senior/solo rabbis. Similarly, the share of women in senior/solo rabbi positions grew in every congregation size category over the same time period. Most of the growth in the female share occurred among the smallest congregations (an increase of 6 percentage points). But, given that rabbis can serve in senior positions in larger congregations as they obtain more experience,[12] an increase of women serving smaller congregations may point towards progress in the future.

In addition to the greater female representation over time, the ACC and ECE-RJ data contribute to the case for optimism regarding female representation and overall pay equity. The ACC data on cantors allows for a similar analysis by position and congregation size. In stark contrast to the senior/solo rabbi position, which is 30 percent female, the senior/solo cantor position is 67 percent female. Given that women make up 67 percent of all cantors (at least among the survey respondents), this means that higher paying cantorial positions do not suffer from underrepresentation of women. Moreover, women are proportionately represented across congregation sizes: both small (250 or less) and large (1,000 or more) congregations have approximately 70 percent female cantors. Notably, a similar pattern of proportional representation was reported in Gould (2018), signifying that female representation has been maintained over time.

Analogous analysis can be performed in the ECE-RJ and ARJE data, bearing in mind that women make up almost the entire ECE-RJ sample. Comparing across different specific occupations—preschool director, director of lifelong learning, assistant director, teacher, and assistant teacher—women are slightly overrepresented (relative to the overall share of women represented in the ECE-RJ data) in all positions except for assistant teacher. Similarly, according to the ARJE data, women are either proportionately represented or overrepresented in positions such as director of education, religious school principal, and assistant director. Moreover, the men and women surveyed report being roughly equally likely to supervise others in their role, the type of responsibility that is likely to correlate with pay. Note that the NATA data do not show the fraction of women for temple administrators and executive directors separately, but rather across the entire sample as a whole (as reported in Table 1). Thus, further analysis of these positions cannot be completed.

In summary, while men still make up the majority of the highest paying rabbinical positions, there has been meaningful progress towards female representation. Insofar as this leads to higher paychecks for women, this is ultimately progress towards closing the gender gap in earnings. With this context in mind, the next section turns to wage and earnings gaps *within* occupations.

## Gender Inequality in Salary Within Occupations

Having established how men and women sort across various roles within the Reform Movement, a natural next step is to analyze how pay differs by gender within those roles. In making these comparisons, it is important to underscore the data limitations here in particular. Even when comparing men and women's salaries within a role, things like number of hours worked, assigned responsibility, experience, and so on may differ by gender—yet many of these characteristics are unobserved in the available data. The conclusion discusses this in more detail. Regardless, the basic story remains that men tend to earn more than women across many of the occupations. Overall, there is some evidence for progress since the Gould (2018) report, while other evidence suggests there is still much room for improvement.

Across all senior/solo rabbis, the gender gap in annual base salary is 16 percent ($186,120 versus $156,767) on average. The gap is much smaller when comparing salaries by gender within different congregation size categories. This confirms the discussion from the previous section that men's relatively higher propensity to be in larger congregations drives up earnings inequality. However, while men are more likely to be in larger congregations, the gender gap decreases with congregation size, a pattern that was also present in the Gould (2018) report. This suggests that future programming for pay equity could target smaller congregations. The gender gap in base salary for senior/solo rabbis in congregations with 300 or fewer members is 8 percent ($125,919 versus $115,908), for congregations with 301–599 members is 9 percent ($179,096 versus $163,365), and for congregations with at least 600 members is 4 percent ($274,896 versus $262,607). While pay inequities still exist, the gender gap has decreased substantially in two of three congregation size categories since Gould (2018), where the gap was 13 percent, 9 percent, and 8 percent, respectively.

Among associate rabbis, the gender gap in annual base salary is 12 percent ($160,502 versus $141,886) on average. This is larger than the gap reported in Gould (2018). In contrast, the gender gap has closed (and perhaps even reversed) for assistant rabbis, suggesting that some progress has been made over time. In Gould (2018), female assistant rabbis earned 4 percent less, while in the current data, women earn slightly more than men ($109,365 versus $107,976). The relatively small number of associate rabbis and assistant rabbis does not allow for breaking down the gender gap for these occupations by the same congregation size categories.

Across the three categories of rabbinic positions, men make on average 18 percent more than women ($176,862 versus $145,239). This is a slight improvement over the 19 percent gap report in Gould (2018). When rabbi educators are included in the data set, however, men make 20 percent more on average than women ($174,061 versus $139,085). There is no comparable measurement in the Gould report.

The ACC data allow for a richer analysis of disparities in base salary by gender among cantors. Across all cantor respondents, on average, men make 14 percent more than women ($170,975 versus $146,195). This masks substantial variation in the gap across congregation size. Larger congregations exhibit wider gender gaps in salary, as depicted in the right panel of Figure 2, where the gap widens to 29 percent among the largest congregations. In contrast, the gap is nearly nonexistent in congregations of 251–500 members. This suggests that, in contrast to rabbi pay disparities, programming aimed at closing salary gaps among cantors may be most useful in larger congregations. Notably, these gaps are either the same (or slightly larger) than the gaps reported in Gould (2018), suggesting that further work ought to be done to fulfill the social justice mandate of pay equity across gender.

Figure 2 also breaks down the gap across cantors' experience at a given congregation. This reveals only modest variation, with gaps tending to be slightly smaller among more experienced individuals. Nevertheless, the gap is never smaller than 10 percent, suggesting that differences in experience is not a primary driver of pay inequity among cantors. Comparing these gaps to Gould (2018), gender gaps among the more experienced closed while gaps among less experienced cantors increased slightly.

Because only 12 men (out of 502 total respondents) are included in the ECE-RJ sample, analysis of the salary gap is omitted.

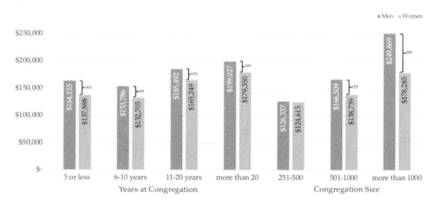

Figure 2: Cantor pay by gender

*Note:* Source is ACC 2019 data

However, the ARJE data give a sense of pay disparities among educators in the Reform Movement. On average, across respondents in the ARJE, men tend to earn slightly more than women yielding a gender gap of 6 percent in base salary ($99,522 versus $93,061). This stays relatively stable when zooming into directors of education (full-time) specifically, where women earn 7.5 percent less than their male counterparts ($94,382 versus $102,065).

Only a very crude salary comparison comes from NATA, which simply reports the average and quartiles of base salary by gender. On average, the women in this sample earn 18 percent less than men ($99,656 versus $121,066), roughly the same amount as reported in Gould (2018). Interestingly, the gap at the third quartile is *smaller* than the gap at the first quartile (15 percent versus 21 percent). However, it is difficult to interpret these statistics further without observing salaries by gender across other characteristics. For instance, the base salary across all respondents increases sharply with the operating budget of the temple. Therefore, it could be the case that men in this sample are more likely to be at larger synagogues, and thus receive higher pay. Alternatively, it could be that men and women systematically choose different specific occupations within temple administration, thus explaining the gap. Without more data, it is not possible to disentangle which factors are behind the gender gap.

In short, pay disparities are largest among rabbis, cantors, and temple administrators. While female rabbis are less likely to serve as senior/solo rabbis at larger congregations, the gender gap narrows with congregation size. In contrast, the gap widens with congregation size among cantors. In cases where comparison over time is possible, gender gaps grew in some cases and closed in others. In particular, salaries have become more gender equal among rabbis, regardless of congregation size. Among cantors, however, pay gaps have either stayed relatively steady or slightly increased.

## Parental Leave

Women often face the challenge of juggling childcare or maternity leave with their careers. A potentially important job amenity is thus parental leave, which eases the burden of taking a break from work during the early stages of motherhood. In fact, women may be willing to take a slight salary decrease in exchange for maternal leave (especially if it is paid), and thus the presence of this amenity could help explain pay disparities. Analyzing whether this is true is outside of the scope of this analysis. Nevertheless, this short section describes the state of unpaid and paid parental leave for the occupations that reported data on the subject.

Among cantors, 72 percent of full-time pulpit respondents of both genders report being contractually entitled to maternity/paternity leave, the vast majority (97 percent) of whom further report that the leave is paid. On average, parental leave lasts 63 days (9 weeks) for this group of respondents. Women are more likely to have access to parental leave (78 percent of female respondents versus 57 percent of males). In contrast, only 32 percent of cantors in limited-service pulpit positions report parental leave (80 percent of which is paid). These lower rates are more typical of other Jewish professionals' access across the Reform Movement. Only 27.5 percent of early childhood educator respondents in the ECE-RJ—the majority of whom are women—report having parental leave, but it is unclear from the data whether it is paid. The average number of days allowed is 44.4. Among ARJE respondents, 35 percent report having access to paid parental leave at full salary with an average number of days of 54. Similarly, 36 percent of the temple administrators reported have parental leave with an average number of days allowed of 49, although it is once again unclear whether the leave is paid.

Drawn from administrative data, the CCAR data does not document family and medical leave. However, a constituent organization of the CCAR, the Women's Rabbinic Network, conducted a family leave survey of their membership, which is comprised of female-identified Reform rabbis.[13] In the WRN family and medical leave survey data, 23.5 percent of responding rabbis reported receiving paid parental leave as part of their contract with an average length of leave of 9.7 weeks. In addition, 34.6 percent of respondents reported they received paid family medical leave, with an average leave length of 4.2 weeks.[14] Medical leave data was not available from the other organizations.

In summary, there is modest leave access across the Reform Movement among the occupations studied, with full-time pulpit cantors reporting the most generous amount of paid leave and educators reporting the lowest. Interestingly, the gender gap in salary among cantors is higher than those in education occupations. While this suggests that lower pay could be compensating for access to this amenity, the fact that temple administrators have both a relatively high gender gap in salary and only modest access to leave (which may or may not be paid) suggests otherwise. In any case, further research with more granular data, especially on *paid* leave, could study this further.

## Next Steps and Conclusions

Data on occupational sorting and salaries for rabbis, cantors, educators, and administrators across the Reform Movement suggest that women still face barriers to equality. Women tend to be found in lower paying careers and when they do enter the higher paying occupations, they tend to be in smaller congregations or lower paying positions. While this highlights the pervasiveness of occupational gender segregation, the progress over time in female representation (relative to Gould [2018]) is encouraging. The data still reveal what appear to be meaningful gaps in earnings between men and women across occupations, especially among rabbis, cantors, and administrators. There is mixed evidence of progress over the past couple of years. Rabbi pay has trended towards equality while the cantor pay gap remained roughly constant. However, when it comes to parental leave (a valuable job amenity for many women), cantors in full-time pulpit positions appear to have the most generous access, while rabbinical, educational, and administrative occupations have relatively less access.

The data limitations discussed earlier suggest a few concrete next steps for the RPEI as they continue to address this issue. Data collection for the survey data would be greatly improved by reducing non-response rates and/or engaging in random sampling in order to obtain a representative survey. Additionally, if any administrative data sets (like the CCAR) exist, they could be used in place of the surveys or at least a subset of the survey questions. Finally, survey questionnaires could be improved by using the thorough set of questions in the ACC as a guide for what questions to include.

The progress since Gould (2018) ought to send a hopeful message. This confirms that solutions are within reach. To continue making progress, the Reform Movement could consider interviewing women across different occupations (e.g., associate rabbi) and asking what barriers they tend to face in succeeding in their careers. A subset of targeted questions could be based on recent academic research (such as in Blau and Kahn [2017]) summarizing the main drivers of gender inequality in the labor market.[15] For example, part of the interview could ask whether women felt they could easily juggle family or childcare responsibilities and their work and, if not, what sorts of things would help them accomplish this better. These sorts of insights could inform the ongoing interventions aimed at closing the gaps further.

## Notes

1. "Pay Equity Within the Reform Movement" (symposium), *CCAR Journal* (Fall 2018), https://www.ccarnet.org/the-reform-jewish-quarterly-fall-2018/.
2. Amanda Barroso and Anna Brown, "Gender Pay Gap in U.S. Held Steady in 2020," Pew Research Center (2021), https://www.pewresearch.org/fact-tank/2021/05/25/gender-pay-gap-facts/.
3. Shulamit Kahn and Donna Ginther, "Women and STEM," working paper no. 23525, National Bureau of Economic Research (June 2017), https://www.nber.org/system/files/working_papers/w23525/w23525.pdf.
4. Michela Carlana, "Implicit Stereotypes: Evidence from Teachers' Gender Bias," *Quarterly Journal of Economics* 134, no. 3 (2019): 1163–1224.
5. Barbara Biasi and Heather Sarsons, "Flexible Wages, Bargaining, and the Gender Gap," forthcoming in *The Quarterly Journal of Economics* (published online August 16, 2021), https://doi.org/10.1093/qje/qjab026.
6. Claudia Goldin, "A Grand Gender Convergence: Its Last Chapter," *American Economic Review* 104, no. 4 (2014): 1091–1119.
7. This article only breaks down gender by male and female. Unfortunately, there is not enough data to include analysis on nonbinary/gender fluid individuals.
8. Elise Gould, "The Gender Wage Gap in the Reform Movement: A United Data Narrative," *CCAR Journal* (Fall 2018): 48–59.
9. For example, the ACC and NATA surveys received response rates of 55.3 percent and 78 percent, respectively.
10. The CCAR data covers rabbi educators as well as rabbis. When including rabbi educators in this statistic, 40 percent of all rabbis and rabbi educators are women.
11. Gould, "The Gender Wage Gap."
12. CCAR Handbook for Placement Procedures can be found at https://www.ccarnet.org/placement-and-transition/placement-documents/.

13. The WRN family and medical leave survey is currently unpublished. It was conducted by The Center for Parental Leave Leadership under the direction of Dr. Amy Beacom and Dr. Amy Pytlovany.

14. WRN has created the resource "Family and Medical Leave: Policy Standards for the Jewish Community," to advance paid family and medical leave for all employees. The WRN recommends a standard of twelve weeks of paid leave. The resource can be found at https://womensrabbinicnetwork.org/Family-Leave.

15. Francine D. Blau and Lawrence M. Kahn, "The Gender Wage Gap: Extent, Trends, and Explanations," *Journal of Economic Literature* 55, no. 3 (2017): 789–865.

# T'filat HaAdam and the Maturation of Israeli Reform

*Michael Rosen and Rabbi David Ellenson, PhD*

### Introductory Remarks

Reform Judaism burst onto the scene of history in Germany as a movement of liturgical reform. In 1819, the Hamburg Temple published a *Gebetbuch* that expressed the ideals of the Reformers in embryonic form. However, as the late historian Steven Lowenstein has indicated, it was not until the 1840s with the "maturation of the Reform Movement," that more mature expressions of a principled Reform as manifest in pamphlets and prayer books began to emerge.[1]

In a parallel vein, it can be said that with the 2020 publication of *T'filat HaAdam: Siddur Reformi Yisraeli*, co-edited by Rabbah Dalia Marx and Rabbah Alona Lisitsa and released under the aegis of MARAM (the Israeli Progressive Rabbinical Council) and the Israeli Reform Movement, that Reform Judaism in Israel, like the German movement of the 1840s, has begun fully to come of age. To be sure, *HaAvodah SheBaLev*, the 1982 siddur of the Israeli Movement for Progressive Judaism, which was revised in 1991 under the editorship of Rabbi Yehoram Mazor, constitutes a significant Israeli Reform liturgical antecedent for *T'filat HaAdam*. As the eminent historian of modern Jewish liturgy Eric Friedland indicated, in his "Ha-Avodah sheba-Lev (1982): A Siddur from Zion," this prayer book constituted a major step in the advancement of Reform Judaism in Israel, and Rabbi Mazor and Rabbi Esther Adler discussed the character and significance of this work in the pages of this journal in 1993.[2]

MICHAEL ROSEN is a consultant in the financial services industry and married to Rabbi Karen Fox.

RABBI DAVID ELLENSON, PhD (NY77) is chancellor emeritus of HUC-JIR and recently co-authored, with Rabbi Michael Marmur, *American Jewish Thought Since 1934: Writings on Identity, Engagement, and Belief* (Brandeis University Press, 2020).

In this article, we certainly acknowledge the importance of *HaAvodah SheBaLev* as a precedent for *T'filat HaAdam*. The editors themselves indicate that the text they employed as the basis for their siddur was the earlier 1982 Israeli siddur.[3] At the same time, we maintain that the current iteration of Reform prayer in Israel unquestionably testifies to a giant leap forward in the growth of Israeli Reform over the past four decades. *T'filat HaAdam* bespeaks a self-confidence and maturity that marks contemporary Reform Judaism in Israel as it enters the third decade of the twenty-first century. It is that "leap forward" and what it says about Israeli Reform Judaism today that we wish to explore in this article.

At the outset, we would note that this prayer book is the product of an historical context that is much different than the one that produced *HaAvodah SheBaLev*. Liberal expressions of Judaism now occupy a much more prominent position on the Israeli scene than they did forty years ago. Surveys conducted under the aegis of the Avi Chai Foundation in 2011 and The Jewish People Policy Institute in 2019 found that 13 percent of Israeli Jews (800,000 persons) identify themselves as Reform and Conservative; 60 percent of all Israeli Jews believe that the Reform and Conservative Movements should be recognized by the State and that their rabbis should be allowed to perform legally sanctioned marriages; and 34 percent said they had attended a ceremony or service where a non-Orthodox rabbi had officiated and the Israeli Reform and Masorti movements report that they conduct approximately 3,500 bar or bat mitzvah ceremonies as well as 1,200 weddings each year.[4]

While these movements do not enjoy a large formal membership, the number of Reform and Masorti congregations have multiplied exponentially over past decades. Reform alone has jumped from eleven Reform congregations in Israel in 1982 to fifty-four today. In addition, fifteen Reform rabbis today as opposed to zero then now receive Israeli governmental support, and TALI schools under Reform aegis are providing an enriched Jewish curriculum for secular Israeli Jewish students throughout the country. Furthermore, in a landmark decision issued on March 1, 2021, the Israeli Supreme Court ruled in *Natalia Dahan and Others v. The Minister of the Interior and Others* (HCJ 11013/05) that persons converted to Judaism by Reform and Conservative rabbinical courts in Israel must be granted Israeli citizenship under the Law of Return. Equally noteworthy is that Rabbi Gilad Kariv, past head of the

Israel Movement for Progressive Judaism, now sits as a member of the Knesset. Finally, more than one hundred Israelis were ordained as Reform and Masorti Rabbis during the first years of the twenty-first century by Hebrew Union College and Machon Schechter in Jerusalem.[5]

Among these rabbis are Rabbis Marx and Lisitsa. Marx, a tenth generation Israeli, was ordained at HUC-JIR Jerusalem and Cincinnati in 2002 and completed her doctorate in Midrash at Hebrew University. Rabbah Marx, the Rabbi Aaron D. Panken Professor of Midrash and Liturgy at HUC-JIR/Jerusalem, is a prolific author and lecturer who writes and speaks in Hebrew, English, German, and Spanish. Her fame is now pronounced in both Israel and throughout the world. Similarly, Lisitsa, born in Kiev and ordained at HUC-JIR/Jerusalem in 2004, also teaches at HUC-JIR/Jerusalem, serving as Coordinator of Student Placement for the Israeli Rabbinic Program. Lisitsa, holder of a 2012 PhD in Talmud from Tel Aviv University, is a full-time adjunct professor of Halachah and Liturgy at the Jerusalem campus of the College-Institute as well. Most notably, she is the editor of *Dabri Torah*, the recently published Israeli Women's Pluralistic Torah Commentary. Together, Lisitsa and Marx embody and guide a proud new generation of Israeli Reform and liberal Jews and serve as catalysts for novel senses of religious and cultural belonging in Israel today. Indeed, this "belonging" is evidenced by the sale of *T'filat HaAdam* in Steimatzky bookstores and others throughout Israel—the first Reform prayer book to ever be sold in this way! In this essay, we will describe how Lisitsa, Marx, and the Israeli Reform Movement have achieved this prominence by presenting and analyzing the character and substance of *T'filat HaAdam*, the Israeli prayer book they and the Reform Movement have birthed.

## The Significance of a Name

For years, Reform Judaism was unknown to most Israelis and the term "Reform" itself had a pejorative connotation on the Israeli scene. The nationalistic elements that informed the Zionist Movement caused the overwhelming majority of Israeli Jews during the first decades of the State to regard the anti-nationalistic stances that informed classical Reform Judaism in both Germany and the United States as a perversion of Judaism. As Eric Yoffie has reported, this led authors of textbooks for Israeli secular schools to present Reform Judaism as an assimilatory movement designed to cast away Jewish identity for upper-class elites in *galut*.[6] The Reform Movement was viewed so negatively by the Israeli Jewish populace that the Israeli Movement abjured the title "Reform," causing an Israeli Reform official, as the late Israeli Conservative Rabbi Theodore Friedman reported in 1982, to regard the term "Reform" as "an albatross around our necks." Indeed, it was Friedman who remarked, "It is revealing that in Israel the movement uses the appellation Progressive Judaism and not Reform."[7]

It is small wonder then that the title of the first Israeli Reform siddur, *HaAvodah SheBaLev*, did not proclaim a connection to the Reform Movement. To be sure, the name of that first prayer book admittedly resonates with both traditional and liberal Jewish tradition. After all, the words in its name are inspired by a passage in *Taanit* 2a, where the Rabbis assert that prayer is defined as "service of the heart." In this sense, *HaAvodah SheBaLev* is akin to numerous other Jewish liturgical works composed over the past two centuries, including the 1967 *Avodat HaLev* of the British Liberal Movement. However, nowhere on the cover or the spine of *HaAvodah SheBaLev* does the term "Reform" or even "liberal" or "progressive" appear—though inside on its third page where the title appears the book does identity itself as affiliated with the Movement for Progressive Judaism in Israel.

This "embarrassment" over the "appellation . . . Reform" is no more. The very subtitle given to *T'filat HaAdam*, "*Siddur Reformi Yisraeli*," testifies to this. The words of the subtitle indicate that the prayer book unapologetically takes great pride in proclaiming its Reform affiliation. From this perspective, the new Israeli Reform siddur is a radical change from its predecessor liturgy as well from both previous traditional siddurim and classical Reform siddurim.

The full name and title page of *T'filat HaAdam: Siddur Reformi Yisraeli* proudly announces its multilayered character to the Israeli audience for which it is intended. It is, in keeping with Reform tradition, literally universalistic—the prayer of humanity.[8] At the same time, it is highly particularistic and unabashedly identifies itself as being "Israeli and Reform," which as Lisitsa observes, means that Reform is committed to both "tradition and innovation" and that it has the courage to proclaim this to the Israeli public and "not bow to external definitions."[9]

As Rabbahs Lisitsa and Marx note in their introduction, for an Israeli audience, the title immediately recalls the Hannah Szenes poem "*Eili, Eili*,"[10] and the poem appears in full as the frontispiece of the work (p. 10). Secondly, by announcing itself on the cover and the binding of the book as well as on its front page as an "Israeli Reform Siddur," *T'filat HaAdam*, in the words of its editors, acknowledges unabashedly that the Israeli Reform Movement has merited great growth in recent decades and that the Movement is both burgeoning and multivalent (p. 13). We will now analyze what the contents of *T'filat HaAdam* say precisely about the nature of Israeli Reform today by looking at it as (1) a prayer book informed by Reform tradition and (2) a siddur that reflects a contemporary Israeli context and feminist sensibilities. All of this will bespeak the nature of Reform Judaism in present-day Israel and testify to the expanded role the Reform Movement occupies in the life and culture of Israel today.[11]

## *T'filat HaAdam* as a Reform Siddur

*T'filat HaAdam* announces itself as a Reform prayer book on its very first page, where it indicates that it is the product of the Israeli Reform Movement and MARAM. Lisitsa and Marx, in their introduction to the siddur, go to great length to indicate that this work is the product of the Reform Movement and sees itself as a link in the chain of Reform Movement siddurim. Rabbah Lisitsa recognizes that while she and Rabbah Marx surely played central roles in the writing of *T'filat HaAdam*, she acknowledges that the siddur is the product of the entire Israeli Reform Movement. They give special thanks to Rabbi Gilad Kariv as head of the IMPJ and the staff of HUC-JIR/ Jerusalem for the contributions and support they provided in the composition of the prayer book. They also acknowledge the help provided by the CCAR and Rabbi Hara Person in the publication and editing of the siddur. Lisitsa and Marx express further gratitude to HUC-JIR/Jerusalem Professor of Modern Jewish Thought Rabbi Yehoyada Amir and their colleagues in MARAM who accompanied them throughout the process of writing this work (p. 15). Indeed, immediately following the preface, Rabbi Amir, on behalf of MARAM and in the name of their partners in the Movement and at HUC, writes a two-page salutation congratulating the co-editors on their accomplishment in composing *T'filat HaAdam* (pp. 16–17).

During the six-year process (2014–2020) that the prayer book was produced, Lisitsa states that the co-editors paid careful "attention to the many diverse voices of the Movement"—its members, its rabbis, its activists, its prayer leaders, and its youth—as the siddur went through numerous iterations. She also notes that careful attention was paid to the many diverse voices teeming in Israeli society, especially its egalitarian prayer groups. Citations of all these influences testify to the dual Reform and Israeli character of *T'filat HaAdam*.[12] Unquestionably, *T'filat HaAdam* is self-consciously a Reform Movement product anchored in the contemporary context of *M'dinat Yisrael* and aims at a broad Israeli as well as Reform audience.

The co-editors emphasize that the Reform heritage of their prayer book is fully evidenced in the structure, characteristics, and substance of the prayer book itself. In their introduction, Lisitsa and Marx note that Reform prayer books throughout history express "the eternal values of the Jewish people" by providing links to past generations. This means that Reform siddurim—and *T'filat HaAdam* is no exception—retain the classical *matbei-ah shel t'filah*, the traditional Rabbinic structure of Jewish prayer. At the same time each Reform siddur seeks to combine those voices of previous generations with the needs of the contemporary community. *T'filat HaAdam* therefore consciously weaves "episodes, understandings and questions that animate our generation" with materials from the past. In this sense, the new Israeli rite unquestionably bears greater similarity to the "moderate" school of Reform siddurim embodied in the liturgical works of Abraham Geiger and Isaac Mayer Wise than in the more "radical" Reform siddurim of Samuel Holdheim, David Einhorn, and the *Union Prayerbook*.[13] Having recognized where *T'filat HaAdam* stands in a two-hundred-year tradition of Reform prayer books, Lisitsa also notes that in the Israeli context the new Reform prayer book can also be described from one perspective as "radical" and from another as "conservative." That is, the Orthodox, she states, view the siddur as "overly creative" and protest its inclusion of non-canonical sources within its pages. At the same time, secular Israelis see its affirmation of classical Jewish prayer structure and services as overly traditional.[14]

In adopting this moderate model for their prayer book, Lisitsa and Marx point out that Reform siddurim have never been of a single cloth.[15] As Israelis, they are quite conscious that classical Reform prayer books of the nineteenth century abjured any connection with Zion. Obviously, *T'filat HaAdam*, like other modern Reform prayer books composed in both Israel and the Diaspora, departs from this posture. At the same time, this iteration of the Reform Israeli siddur, like all Reform prayer books, rejects traditional prayers calling for the restoration of animal sacrifices and the rebuilding of a Third Temple. Furthermore, Lisitsa and Marx indicate their prayer book does not ask for the coming of a personal messiah. Rather, *T'filat HaAdam*, again like other modern Reform liturgies, speaks of social justice and the obligation of *tikkun olam*. While the Israeli rite affirms the unity of the people Israel, it also renounces negative expressions regarding other peoples and omits all traditional prayers that ask for divine vengeance on the enemies of Israel (pp. 10–15).

A representative glance at the contents of *T'filat HaAdam* displays all the qualities that Lisitsa and Marx have outlined in their introduction. The siddur is laid out as a modern Reform siddur. It begins with the *Arvit* service and cycles through the day. Of course, services for Shabbat and Holidays are included, and the new Israeli rite generally follows the table of contents of *HaAvodah SheBaLev*. However, there are also notable distinctions.

For example, while the *Avot* benediction in the *Amidah* reflects the ideological posture of Reform by eliminating the traditional call for a messianic "redeemer" (*go-eil*) in favor of "redemption" (*g'ulah*), the co-editors of *T'filat HaAdam* do not display such ideational purity in relationship to the *Kaddish*. Indeed, the 2020 prayer book always includes two versions of this prayer—the traditional Ashkenazic rite and the traditional Sephardic rite. As is well-known, the Sephardic rite includes a phrase asking for the coming of redemption and a personal messiah: [16]‎ויצמח פרקנה—ויקרב (קץ) משיחה. In placing the Sephardic prayer in their siddur, Lisitsa and Marx show themselves to be worthy heirs of Abraham Geiger, who, as the communal rabbi of Breslau, composed an 1854 *Gebetbuch* that contained several traditional beliefs and ideals with which he personally disagreed. However, as rabbi of the entire community, he included these items in his prayer book for the sake of communal unity.[17] Similarly, Lisitsa and Marx recognize that the need to have a significant prayer that grants comfort to many Israelis is more important than avoiding the "ideological contamination" that a yearning for a personal messiah represents. In so doing, the Rabbis reveal their overarching commitment to the creation of a Reform liturgy that reflects the lived "Jewish experience of" Sephardic/ Mizrachi Jews and their traditions (p. 13).

The sensitivity to Jewish liturgical tradition and the influence the Sephardic/Mizrachi Israeli possesses for the authors can be found in numerous places in *T'filat HaAdam*. The daily *Shacharit* prayer service includes *Tachanun*, which follows the rite of the Nusach Ari/ Sfard and Oriental communities rather than the traditional Ashkenazic rite by including the *Ashamnu* and the thirteen attributes of God in the daily *Tachanun* service. However, in addition to the traditional text, there are modern Hebrew poems as alternative prayers. By including these additions, the newest Israeli Reform rite consciously weaves "episodes, understandings and questions that animate our generation" with materials from the past. The co-editors state that they consciously affirm "metaphorical" readings of their prayer texts and are content to have God understood in a variety of ways by different worshipers. Indeed, they are delighted to have each person and each community construct their own theological approaches to the Divine. The only sources they explicitly excluded from the siddur are ones that are "chauvinistic" or "racist."[18]

*T'filat HaAdam* also adds back *Ashrei* in *P'sukei D'zimrah* and the *piyut El Adon* in the first blessing before the *Sh'ma*. In so doing, the Israeli prayer book follows the lead of other Reform siddurim in the modern era and reflects the spirituality that increasingly marks present-day Jewish religiosity. The Psalms for each day of the week also appear, and in the *Amidah*—in a nod once again to the Sephardic tradition—the alternative version for the winter blessing used by Sephardic rites for the blessing of the seasons (ninth blessing) is found.

The traditionalism of *T'filat HaAdam* manifests itself once again in the Shabbat section of the prayer book, which begins with "preparations for Shabbat" (*Hachanot L'Shabbat*). There are prayers for the separation of *Challah* and *T'rumah* followed by prayers, supplications, and readings drawn from the traditional and modern sources (including readings prepared by kibbutzim and a meditation by Rabbi Leo Baeck) to prepare the Jew for the sanctity and rest of Shabbat. Of course, while this admixture of classical and contemporary sources is an ongoing characteristic of *T'filat HaAdam*, the inclusion of the prayer for *T'rumah* underlines both the traditional as well as Israeli character of this siddur, as *T'rumah* applies only in Israel and would have resonance only with an Israeli audience. Lisitsa also points out that within an Israeli framework the word *t'rumah* also connotes the giving of *tzedakah* in honor of the Sabbath. In this way, the inclusion of *T'rumah* in the siddur allows for innovation and renewal even as it affirms tradition. Once again, the "old-new" character of *T'filat HaAdam* is evidenced.[19]

The emphasis upon traditional forms and prayers in *T'filat HaAdam* is seen in other passages and prayers contained in this prayer book. For example, *Shir HaShirim* (The Song of Songs) is added in its entirety, and the Shabbat Morning Service ends with *Anim Z'mirot*. The inclusion of this mystical poem once again reflects the comfort Israeli Reform Jews feel with this staple of Orthodox worship. *Minchah* for Shabbat has an addition between *Ashrei* and *Uva L'tzion* of several psalms, though *T'filat HaAdam* moves the entire Saturday Afternoon Torah Service from its traditional site between *Uva L'tzion* and the *Amidah*, as does the North American *Mishkan T'filah*, to after the *Amidah*. It also includes the *Shir Hamaalot* psalms as a nod to the *Nusach Ari* with which Ashkenazic Israelis who attend synagogue are familiar. After *Havdalah*, *Kiddush L'vana* (Sanctification of the New Moon) is added to the new Israeli Reform rite. At the same time, following the work of Marcia Falk in *The Book of Blessings*, a special innovative *Kiddush* for Rosh Chodesh based on biblical and Rabbinic sources is found.

Other traditional additions not found in *HaAvodah SheBaLev* should also be highlighted. The appearance of *Tashlich* surely represents a departure from classical Reform prayer books. While this Yom Kippur ritual has long been observed by Reform congregations in Israel, the appearance of the service in the liturgy is novel and is in line with a resurgence of traditional forms in the prayers of contemporary Reform. Tu BiSh'vat has a service, the fast day of 17 Tammuz receives a short prayer, and *Tu B'Av* receives a page. There is a short service for Tzom G'daliah, and the fast of 10 Tevet appears while being reinterpreted as the day to recite *Kaddish* for all the departed who have no one to recite *Kaddish* for them. In so doing, *T'filat HaAdam* follows the reinterpretation of this fast in the Religious Zionist camp. *B'dikat chameitz* is placed in the siddur while Lag BaOmer receives its own very short benediction. All of this testifies to the renewed appreciation for the *Masoret* in contemporary Israeli Reform.

The way that *T'filat HaAdam* includes and treats two traditional prayers—*Aleinu* and *Musaf*—displays the character of how present-day Israeli Reform Judaism affirms the structure of traditional Jewish prayer even as it adapts its manifest content to the principles of Reform thought. The *Aleinu* is retained as it is in countless Reform prayer books. However, the "overbearing" particularity, to quote Abraham Geiger, of those sections in the traditional *Aleinu* that speak negatively of other peoples and religious traditions are removed and two alternative versions of the prayer that express thanks to God for giving Israel the Torah and offering gratitude to God for bringing Israel near to divine service are substituted instead. Here the influence of classical Reform thinkers like Geiger as well as the model of contemporary Reconstructionist prayer are evident. Notably, a completely alternative *Aleinu* taken from Marcia Falk that speaks of the obligation to engage in *tikkun olam* is also included as are two texts by Israeli Reform Rabbi Dan Porat.

*Musaf* is a significant addition to *T'filat HaAdam*. Hearkening back once again to moderate Reform liturgists like Geiger, Wise, and Jastrow in the nineteenth century and unlike all twentieth-century North American Reform siddurim and *HaAvodah SheBaLev*, the current rite includes a full Shabbat, Holiday, and Rosh Chodesh Musaf service. However, in the manner of Conservative Movement prayer books, all passages that ask for the actual restoration of animal sacrifices are excised. To be sure, a short *Zecher L'Musaf*, a short remembrance of the Temple and its sacrifices, is also included as an alternative in the new Reform rite. Nevertheless, the full *Musaf* offered in its pages stands in sharp contrast to *HaAvodah SheBaLev*, where a one page *Zecher L'Musaf* alone is included.

In sum, *T'filat HaAdam* stands proudly in a tradition of moderate Reform prayer books. It affirms the traditions of Jewish worship even as it reflects significant change and evolution from past rites. An analysis of its "Israeli" character and its subsequent attention to personal rites and ceremonies as well as feminist concerns will highlight its distinctiveness. It is to a description of those elements in the siddur that we now turn.

## The Israeli Context and Feminist Sensibilities and Expressions

In assessing the Israeli context of *T'filat HaAdam* and what it says about the nature and growth of the Reform Movement in Israel today, we now turn, perhaps unexpectedly, to an examination of the services and ceremonies it includes for personal rites in the liturgical life cycle of the Israeli Jew. As Friedland pointed out in his commentary on *HaAvodah SheBaLev*, "the excision of services that one would expect as a matter of course in a prayerbook as omnibus as *Ha-Avodah sheba-Lev*: for a *berit milah*, a wedding, and the final rites," was extremely striking. He then observed, "Could it be that the exclusion is due to the situation in Israel today, wherein the Orthodox exercise a virtual monopoly over the central liturgical events in its citizens' personal lives? If so, the absence of such services is a sad commentary."[20]

To be sure, the co-editors of *T'filat HaAdam* acknowledge their indebtedness to *HaAvodah SheBaLev* and they speak reverently about how the 1982 siddur spoke imaginatively to the Israel of its day (p. 15). Furthermore, as Friedland has pointed out in his article on *HaAvodah SheBaLev*, "There is no question that the Israeli experience has etched itself deeply in this prayerbook."[21] There is a service there for Yom HaZikaron, a *Mi Shebeirach* for young people entering the Israel Defense Forces, a service for planting of trees, and a revision of the classical *Al HaNisim* prayer to reflect the "miracle" of a new-born Jewish commonwealth. In that same vein, there is a word change for the benediction in *Birkat HaMazon* of *v'hashleim* ("complete") in lieu of *u'v'nei* ("build") that now asks for the "completion" of the rebuilding of Jerusalem that has already begun to be realized through the creation of the State, and the traditional benedictions relating to *kibbutz galuyot* (ingathering of the exiles) were altered to reflect that many Jews now live in "our land." Hebrew poetry drawn from Israeli secular and religious sources are also found in *HaAvodah SheBaLev*, and a special *Kiddush* for Yom HaAtzma-ut, which we will discuss more fully below, is also placed in the 1982 rite. In short, the earlier Israeli Reform prayer book does bear witness to its Israeli context.

However, forty years later, the contents of *T'filat HaAdam* reflect how changed the position of Reform Judaism is in Israel today from what it was then. To paraphrase Friedland, the appearance of blessings, services, and ceremonies for special occasions in life is a positive commentary on Reform in contemporary Israel despite the ongoing outsized legal influence the *Rabbanut* continues to exercise in the State.[22]

*Mi Shebeirach* prayers for personal occasions abound. They include blessings for *eirusin* and *nisuin*, the dedication of a home, the birth of a son or daughter, adoption, conversion, conscription into the Israel Defense Forces, and birthdays. Meaningful prayers for Yom HaMishpacha are included and other prayers for milestones in life also appear within the pages of this prayer book. There are prayers for *olim* and for meetings with Jewish communities from the Diaspora. The *Mi Shebeirach* prayer for the sick composed by Debbie Freidman is included in Hebrew translation. *T'filat Ha-Adam* also composes a special *Mi Shebeirach* for "chapter ending life events" (*siyum perek b'chayim*) such as divorce, layoffs (*piturim*), or other crises. A unique recognition of the changed reality LGBTQ+ persons experience in Israel and other parts of the world in our day is provided by a special blessing that celebrates "coming out of the closet" (*Mi Shebeirach l'y'tziah haaron*), where the individual is lauded for the "courage" (*ometz*) to declare the nature of their sexuality publicly. Three recently ordained Israeli rabbis —Rabbah Tamar Duvdevani, Rabbah Ayala Sha'ashua-Miron, and Rabbah Michal Ken-Tor—offer alternative versions of *T'filat HaDerech* even as the traditional version of the prayer also appears. Rabbah Marx provides a final prayer at the conclusion of the siddur, "Open for us a gate during the moment of the gate's closing," where she affirms, in the final two lines of her composition, "God create a pure heart for us, and renew a proper spirit within us."

All these prayers reflect the confidence present-day Israeli Reform possesses and indicates the creativity and traditionalism that mark its rabbis and its members. *T'filat HaAdam* echoes and extends *HaAvodah SheBaLev* in offering an even more complete list of the *birchot hanehenin* (blessings upon food, drink, and life cycle) than were published in the earlier Israeli Reform liturgy. To the traditional *b'rachot* of *Hamotzi, shehakol nihyeh bidvaro, hagefen, minei m'zonot, p'ri haadamah, Shehecheyanu*, and *minei v'samim*, blessings for *isvei v'samim*, the rainbow, *chacham harazim* (for when a crowd of Jews is gathered), *hatov v'hameitiv, t'vilah*, and *m'zuzah* are included, as is the general *birchot hamitzvot*, for the commandments.

The religious and cultural-political reality that informs present-day Israel is seen in the way that *T'filat HaAdam* actively seeks to include the various rites of the Jewish people who currently reside in Israel and devotes ample room to contemporary Israeli poetry, song, and creations. Most such sources are Israeli. The notable exceptions are an excerpt of an essay by Leo Baeck, a poem of the Canadian Jewish poet-singer Leonard Cohen, several pieces from the Chasidic master R. Nahman, and one reading by American Conservative Rabbi Jack Riemer. The overwhelming number (perhaps 90 percent) of the alternative readings are Israeli. These non-Israeli readings, of which several pieces are by Marcia Falk, fall into the contemporary categories of feminist or spiritual thought. This inclusion reflects the popularity these fields enjoy in contemporary Israel.

In addition to the inclusion of the Sephardic as well as Ashkenazic *nusach* for *Kaddish* mentioned above, the Sephardic *hashkavah* with *m'nucha n'chonah* is placed alongside the Ashkenazic *Yizkor* with *El Malei* and *Dayan ha-emet* for burial and the remembrance of souls. Mimonah is added as it has moved from a uniquely Moroccan Jewish to an Israeli festive occasion. There is a moving Memorial Day prayer for the assassination of Prime Minister Rabin. Prayers for *Yom* Y'rushalayim are given a universalistic cast that stand in marked contrast to a right wing chauvinistic Israeli appropriation of the day. A special *El Malei* is recited for the Ethiopian Jews who perished on the way to Israel. In addition, a series of readings stress the theme of Jerusalem as a city of peace and reconciliation for Israel.

A comparison of the different treatment accorded Yom HaAtzmaut in *T'filat HaAdam* as opposed to how Israeli Independence Day is treated in *HaAvodah SheBaLev* captures the nature of "Israeliness" that informs Israeli Reform in 2020. With separate rituals for the night and day, the present Israeli liturgy consciously marks the transition from the solemnity of Yom HaZikaron to the joy of Yom HaAtzma-ut with a service of *Havdalah*. There is a specific liturgy and a *Kiddush* to mark the uniqueness of the day.

Of course, *HaAvodah SheBaLev* also contained a *Kiddush* for this holiday that modeled itself—without reference to miracles—after the *Kiddush* for Israeli Independence Day found in the *machzor* of the Orthodox Religious Kibbutz Movement, though it added a biblical prologue (similar in form to *Kiddush* for Shabbat) from Deuteronomy 8:18: "And you will remember Ado-nai since the Divine is the one that gives you the strength to bear arms (לעשׂרת חיל) in fulfillment of the covenant that the Divine swore to your forebears, as is still the case."[23] The *Kiddush* continued with the blessing over wine and concluded with a blessing that states, "Blessed are you

Ado-nai our God, ruler of the Universe, who redeemed us and redeemed our forebears from slavery to freedom, from servitude to redemption, from despair to joy and from mourning to festive days. So should Ado-nai our God bring us in peace and in the future to festivals and pilgrimage holidays. Blessed are you Ado-nai our God who sanctifies Israel and *Yom Ha'atzmaut.*" *Shehecheyanu* was then recited.

The *Kiddush* in *T'filat HaAdam* takes a different tack. It has a prologue from Psalms 126: "A song of ascents. When Ado-nai restores the fortunes of Zion—we see it as in a dream—our mouths shall be filled with laughter, our tongues, with songs of joy. Then shall they say among the nations, 'Ado-nai has done great things for them!' Ado-nai will do great things for us and we shall rejoice. Restore our fortunes, Ado-nai, like watercourses in the Negeb. They who sow in tears shall reap with songs of joy. Though he goes along weeping, carrying the seed-bag, he shall come back with songs of joy, carrying his sheaves."[24] The siddur then continues with the traditional line, "The Divine who restores before us the fallen booth of David and restores our days as in the past. Blessed are you, Ado-nai the redeemer for Israel. May it be your will Ado-nai that our share will be with all the builders of the House of Israel and Jerusalem the Holy City speedily in our days." This *Kiddush* concludes with the blessing over the wine and *Shehecheyanu.*

This *T'filat HaAdam Kiddush* thus moves from the Psalm traditionally said before *Birkat HaMazon* on Shabbat and Festivals to a messianic trope that recalls and asks for the restoration of the House of David. Once more, the Movement sacrifices "ideological purity" for a more traditional line of prayer familiar to the larger Israeli community. Such "inconsistency" surely characterizes the confidence that characterizes the current Israeli Reform Movement.

In concluding our analysis of *T'filat HaAdam*, we focus on its feminist bent. After all, Rabbah Marx and Rabbah Lisitsa are two of the foremost scholars of Rabbinic texts and feminist theory in the world today. That their prayer book would reflect and embody feminist concerns is anticipated. Furthermore, feminist sensibilities in our world today have grown exponentially over the past four decades since *HaAvodah SheBaLev* was written.

To be fair, as Friedland observed of the 1982 rite, "An egalitarianism of sorts" does appear at time in its pages. "For example, in the *mi she-beirakh* blessing offered on behalf of someone and usually beginning formulaically 'May He who blessed our fathers Abraham, Isaac, and Jacob . . . ,' the matriarchs Sarah, Rebekah, Rachel, and Leah are also included." In addition, "The siddur also offers a unique *mi she-berakh* for a person just inducted into the Israeli Defense Forces. It begins, 'May the One who blessed our fighters [long ago] Joshua, David, and Judah, Deborah, Jael, and Judith bless . . . .' The creators of *Ha-Avodah sheba-Lev* also show their non-sexist sensibilities in launching the *birkat ha-mazon* with '*Friends* (rather than the customary *Gentlemen*), let us say grace.' And they dutifully emulate the official rite of the Israeli Orthodox rabbinate's placement of a feminine *modah* alongside the fixed masculine *modeh* for the familiar *modeh ani* prayer upon arising in the morning."[25]

Yet, as Marx had noted in 2009, "It would be fair to say that until" the Hebrew publication of Aliza Lavie's book, *A Jewish Woman's Prayer Book*, in 2005, "more than a decade after it became a central issue for North American Jewry!, questions of gender and worship were not present on the broader agenda of the Israeli public." Marx contended that little attention was paid to gendered language despite the writings of North American feminists like Falk prior to the issuance of Lavie's work. Of course, Marx also acknowledged that the gendered nature of Hebrew made the task of creating gender-neutral forms in prayer more difficult than in a language like English. Furthermore, she conceded that Israelis often resonate positively to the "feeling" and "authenticity" of the classical liturgy even as they find its manifest content and non-egalitarian imagery troubling.[26]

As a result, Marx maintained, "When it comes to liturgical texts, contemporary Hebrew speakers must constantly choose between the comfort of familiar liturgical practice and the luxury of adequate ideological, theological, and aesthetic text theory. This makes their task quite complicated and at the same time extremely interesting. The discussions around these issues that are most passionate in Israel are those dealing with God language—the ways God is depicted and referred to in the prayers." Thus, "there are no less than four dimensions of reference to gender in the liturgy of Israeli liberal movements, God language being only one of them: 1. Use of inclusive language to refer to worshipers; 2. Addition of representative female characters; 3. Reclaiming and adapting old rituals, creating new rituals and new ritual opportunities; 4. Gender inclusive and gender-balanced metaphors for God."[27]

*T'filat HaAdam* granted Rabbahs Marx, Lisitsa, and the Israeli Reform Movement the opportunity to construct a Movement-wide liturgy that could incorporate these four feminist mandates while addressing a broad Israeli public sensitive to these issues. This siddur is committed to complete equality between all genders and both female and male language is always employed when speaking of persons and addressing worshipers. Feminine images of God abound in its pages even as masculine images are not completely forsaken. God is not only *Adonai*, but *Shechinah*. The Matriarchs are included with the Patriarchs of the Jewish people in every prayer. In the ritual for *ushpizin* on Sukkot, the guests include the female spouses of the traditional male *ushpizin* guests. *Taanit Esther* is expanded to a fast for all *agunot* and women who are being denied a *get*.

## Final Thoughts

*T'filat HaAdam* bespeaks the self-assurance and pride of Reform Judaism in Israel today. It contains the prayers of the different *eidot* (communities) in Israel and displays the rich prayer traditions of the Jewish people throughout history. By presenting a wide and rich range of options, Rabbah Lisitsa and Rabbah Marx make it possible for each community and individual to hew their own paths in prayer even as they create a common liturgy for all. This siddur is a significant achievement for which the editors and the Israeli Movement deserve congratulations. It constitutes, in the words of Rabbah Marx, "testimony to the 'Israeliization' of the Reform Movement" in present-day Israel.[28] This contemporaneous Israeli rite reflects a definition of Jewishness and an aspiration to address a broad swath of the Israeli public in keeping with the ideals and positions that mark the liberal Jewish community in twenty-first-century Israel.

## Notes

1. Steven Lowenstein, "The 1840s and the Creation of the German-Jewish Religious Reform Movement," in Lowenstein, *The Mechanics of Change: Essays in the Social History of German Jewry* (Atlanta: Scholars Press, 1992), 85–131.

2. See Eric Friedland, "Ha-Avodah sheba-Lev (1982): A Siddur from Zion," in Friedland, *Were Our Mouths Filled with Song: Studies in Liberal Jewish Liturgy* (Cincinnati: Hebrew Union College Press,

1997), 259–68. See also Esther Adler-Rephan, "The Reform Movement Has Made 'Aliyah': *Ha-avodah Shebalev* as Its *'Teudat Zehut'*: An Examination of the Israeli Reform Prayerbook," and Yehoram Mazor, "Response," *CCAR Journal* 40, no. 3 (1993): 21–37.

3. Rabbah Lisitsa stated this in an email she sent us on August 24, 2021.

4. Information in this paragraph is taken from David Ellenson, "'Jewishness' in Israel: Israel as a Jewish State," in *Essential Israel: Essays for the 21st Century,* ed. S. Ilan Troen and Rachel Fish (Bloomington: Indiana University Press, 2017), 272–79. On the number of Israeli Jews self-identifying as Reform and Conservative, see http://jppi.org.il/en/article/aa2019/reports/reformconservative/#.YL6Sn0wpCUm, accessed on June 7, 2021. Finally, we thank David Bernstein, Deputy Director General of the Israel Movement for Progressive Judaism, for the information he provided on Reform in Israel in an email sent on June 15, 2021.

5. On the *Dahan* case, see Nicole Maor and David Ellenson, "'Who Is a Convert': The Law of Return and the Legality of Reform and Conservative Conversions in Israel," in *Israel Studies* (forthcoming).

6. Eric H. Yoffie, "Israeli Textbooks on Reform Judaism and Orthodoxy," *Journal of Reform Judaism* (Spring 1983): 94–101.

7. Theodore Friedman, "Projections for Reform and Conservatism in Israel," *Judaism* (Fall 1982): 414.

8. Lisitsa and Marx are sensitive to the fact that for a non-native Hebrew speaking audience the title of their siddur, *T'filat HaAdam,* might appear to be "sexist." As Marx remarks in an as-yet-unpublished paper, "*T'filat HaAdam*: An Israeli Reform Prayer Book" in *Israeli Reform Judaism* (tentative title), ed. Elazar Ben-Lulu and Ofer Shiff (Be'er Sheva: Ben Gurion University, forthcoming) (Hebrew), "There are those who criticize the title [for its use of *Adam*] and contend that it is a gendered word that excludes women." Yet, she observes that the word *adam* first appears in Genesis 1, and there the word is defined as "male and female." Hence, she concludes that the word connotes all humankind and is beyond gender. **Most significantly, in email communications with us on August 24, 2021, both Rabbah Lisitsa and Rabbah Marx assert that native Israeli Hebrew speakers understand *adam* as in fact denoting "humanity," not "male" or "man."** For this reason, they approvingly report that Rabbi Lawrence Hoffman translates the title of *T'filat HaAdam* as "The Prayer that Makes Us Human!" This understanding "allows us to assert the 'universalistic' nature of the title as 'the prayer of humanity.'" We thank both Rabbahs Marx and Lisitsa for sharing their thoughts on this question with us and express our appreciation to Rabbah Marx for

sharing her article, *"T'filat HaAdam: Siddur Yisraeli Reformi,"* with us. For a full discussion in English of gender issues the co-editors confronted in completing *T'filat HaAdam*, see Dalia Marx, *"T'fillat Haadam:* A New Reform Siddur from Israel," *Connection: Newsletter of the Reconstructionist Rabbinical Association* (Late Spring 2021 / Sivan 5781): 1, 11–12.

9. Alona Lisitsa, personal email communication to the authors on August 25, 2021.

10. To be exact, the formal title of the poem is *"Halichah l'keisaria."*

11. Interestingly, even the 2015 Reform *machzor* for the pilgrimage festivals, *HaSimchah SheBalev*, does not explicitly cite its Reform affiliation.

12. Lisitsa describes these influences and the circles that informed the prayer book in her article, *"Tefilat Ha-Orchot,"* in *Midrash Rabah: Ha-rabanut ha-nashit ha-reformit b'yisrael* (tentative title), ed. Maya Leibowitz and Yehoyada Amir (Maram, forthcoming) (Hebrew). Marx speaks of them as well as the time frame required to produce the siddur in her *"T'filat HaAdam."* Once again, we thank both Lisitsa and Marx for sharing their articles with us.

13. On the differences between the "moderate" wing of "classical Reform" as represented by Geiger and Wise and the more "radical" approach championed by Holdheim and Einhorn, see Jakob Petuchowski, "Abraham Geiger and Samuel Holdheim: Their Differences in Germany and Repercussions in America," *Leo Baeck Institute Year Book* XXII (1977): 139–59. David Ellenson delineates these ideological distinctions in their prayer books in "Reform Judaism in Nineteenth Century America: The Evidence of the Prayerbooks," in Ellenson, *Between Tradition and Culture: The Dialectics of Modern Jewish Religion and Identity* (Atlanta: Scholars Press, 1994), 179–96.

14. Lisitsa, personal email communication to the authors on August 25, 2021.

15. For a full statement and description of how Rabbah Marx conceptualizes the characteristics of Reform Jewish Prayer, see Dalia Marx, "Prayer in the Reform Movement: Then and Now," in *A Life of Meaning: Embracing Reform Judaism's Sacred Path*, ed. Dana Kaplan (New York: CCAR Press, 2017), 349–68.

16. In email correspondence with us on August 24, 2021, Rabbah Marx noted that the word *keitz* was purposefully inserted here in this formula to indicate "that a messianic era, and not necessarily a personal messiah" was being emphasized. She further observed that while this word does not appear in most Sephardic renditions of this prayer, it is found in several Chasidic *nuschaot*. Finally, Marx pointed out that the word *keitz* appears in gray, meaning that it is optional for those who pray to decide whether to include

it or not. In this way, she continues, "We [Rabbah Lisitsa and I] attempted to balance theological and sociological [concerns]."

17. For the "ideological inconsistency" Geiger displayed in his own prayer book, see David Ellenson, "The *Israelitische Gebetbücher* of Abraham Geiger and Manuel Joel," in Ellenson, *After Emancipation* (Cincinnati: Hebrew Union College Press, 2004), 208.

18. Lisitsa, personal email communication to us on August 25, 2021.

19. Lisitsa, personal email communication to us on August 25, 2021.

20.. Friedland, *Were Our Mouths Filled with Song*, 265.

21. Friedland, *Were Our Mouths Filled with Song*, 260.

22. Lisitsa and Marx report to us in personal email communications of August 25, 2021, that "the dream" of the Israeli Reform Movement is to compose an entire volume devoted to the life cycle in the near future.

23. The JPS translation of this verse differs from what we offer in our article, but we think that this is the meaning imputed to the verse when used here.

24. JPS translation.

25. Friedland, *Were Our Mouths Filled with Song*, 261–62.

26. Dalia Marx, "Feminist Influences on Jewish Liturgy: The Case of Israeli Reform Prayer," *Sociological Papers* 14: *Women in Israeli Judaism* (Bar Ilan University, 2009), 68ff.

27. Marx, "Feminist Influences," 77.

28. Marx, "*T'filat HaAdam*: An Israeli Reform Prayer Book."

# Experiencing God's Care

*Rabbi Adam D. Fisher*

## 1. The Problem

We have often heard phrases that God cares for us or that God loves us. A few examples from the siddur will suffice: All the morning blessings that *Mishkan T'filah* calls "Blessing for Daily Miracles" assume God's care.[1] Several passages in *P'sukei D'zimrah* such as "Blessed is the One who is compassionate towards all creatures"[2] speak of God's care. There are dozens of passages throughout the siddur with many similar statements such as: "*Adonai* is good to all"[3] and "How deeply you have loved us *Adonai*."[4]

These statements may trouble us. We may not feel that God cares for us personally. We experience and see so much suffering that we have doubts about God's care. We may see that God provides food for all creatures but also the suffering and death that brings to other creatures. The system is based on creatures consuming other creatures in order to survive.[5] Still, we want to feel that God cares what happens to us, that in some sense God loves us and cares for us. And, we wonder if that is true and if so in what sense is it true?

## 2. The Word "God" as a Metaphor and God's Presence

We begin with understanding the word "God." The problem is that the word "God" is a noun but God is not a thing. The biblical use of *yod-hei-vav-hei* or *YHVH* or "was-is-will be," is an impossible noun-verb.[6]

Because of the difficulty in understanding that word and because it is itself a metaphor,[7] the Bible and later Jewish tradition use a variety of metaphors. Some of them are deeply personal such

RABBI ADAM D. FISHER (NY67), DHL (NY71), rabbi emeritus of Temple Isaiah, Stony Brook, New York, is the author of numerous articles and two books of liturgy: *Seder Tu Bishevat* and *An Everlasting Name*. He is also the author of a book of short fiction for children, two Jewish educational works, and four books of poetry. He was the poetry editor of the *CCAR Journal* from 2006 to 2014.

as the medieval poem, *Anu Amecha* ("We are Your People"), which we read on the High Holy Days. It contains the verse: *Anu rayatecha v'atah dodeinu* ("We are Your beloved; and You are our Lover.").[8] It is also translated as "We are Your beloved, You are our Friend."[9] Because God is undefinable and unknowable, all of these and the many other personal ways of addressing God are appropriate if they are understood as metaphors—expressions of our sense of God's Presence at that moment but saying nothing about God.

The one that resonates with me most is *chayeh haolamim* ("the life of all worlds") as that which infuses everything and upholds it and makes it what it is. For those who think in terms of the immanence and transcendence of God, the personal experience of awe and wonder leading to a sense of God's Presence might be thought of in terms of God's immanence, but the metaphor *chayeh haolamim* ("the life of all worlds") also points to transcendence. Menachem Nachum of Chernobyl puts it this way, "The revealed itself also contains the hidden, for the divine essence is the life-force within the revealed."[10]

While I believe that I have felt God's Presence, my encounter with God's Presence has been mostly in encounters with nature. I think of the world as God's garment as the meditation before putting on a tallit says, "You are robed in glory and majesty,/ wrapping Yourself in light as a garment,/spreading forth the heavens like a curtain."[11]

I have been in awe as I view those "garments"—the entry way to God's Presence. As Yoel S. (he does not supply a surname) says, "All we need to do is to uncover the divine from the numerous 'garments' which obscure it from view."[12] I have been in awe at how trees grow and how the trees in a forest interact. I have been speechless and in awe before the indescribable color of hydrangea petals. I have stood in wonder at the sea and watched the waves move toward shore, peak and thunder down, their colors changing from darkest green to jade to white froth. And, I take this wonder and awe as the gateway to God's Presence. Abraham Joshua Heschel helps us understand awe and its relationship to God. He says, "Awe is a way of being in rapport with the mystery of all reality. The awe that we sense . . . when standing in the presence of a human being is a moment of intuition of the likeness of God."[13] He further explains, "Awe, then, is more than a feeling it is an answer of the heart and mind to the presence of mystery in all things, *an intuition for a meaning that is beyond mystery,* an awareness of the *transcendent worth of the universe.*"[14] He ties this to God: "There is no concern for God in the absence of awe."[15] Or expressed in another way: "Awe is a sense for the transcendence, for the reference everywhere to Him who is beyond all things . . . Awe enables us to perceive in the world intimations of the divine."[16]

What follows is my attempt to find an awareness of God's care. We will cover:

- God's care as metaphor
- Human beings in God's image
- Feeling God's care personally
- Consciousness
- Feeling God's care through other people including a discussion of *malachim*
- *K'dushah*
- Torah given in love
- Redemption as an expression of God's care

### 3. Toward an Awareness of God's Care: Metaphor

There are several senses in which we might use the anthropomorphism that "God cares for us," which is to say that we feel God's Caring Presence, which is a metaphor. When we speak of God's caring all we are saying is that we have felt a caring presence that we attribute to God. It may evoke the metaphor, "How deeply You have loved us *Adonai*, our God, gracing us with surpassing compassion!"[17] It says nothing about God who cannot be known. Rather, it is our expression that we have an experience of caring that we attribute ultimately to God. This is similar to awe, which may lead us to God's Presence, and we may evoke the metaphor for God's creative power: "How numerous are Your works, *Adonai*/In wisdom you have formed them all."[18] This is a personal truth.

This is a qualitatively different kind of truth, a personal truth, a personal resonance, which is very different from scientific truth. Lawrence Hoffman makes this clear, "Theology is just not amenable to empirical debate. It is a different category."[19] Arthur Green says it differently, "I begin with an assertion that there's something irreducibly real about religious experience, in all its many 'varieties' . . . It cannot be dismissed as merely an effect of measurable brain wave patterns or as a projection of social norms. Yes, the tools of both physical and social science may help us understand the inner life, but they do not exhaust its truth."[20]

What follows are several ways, situations, instances in which we may feel God's caring presence. We may not feel them all but some of them may resonate with our own experience.

### Consciousness

When I experience awe at the realization that I am a conscious being and I also sense that my consciousness comes from beyond me, I use the metaphor of God or *chayeh haolamim* to express that sense.

One occasion when this occurs for me is the wonder of going to sleep and being unconscious for a period of time and then awakening and regaining consciousness. I know that this can be explained by certain chemical and physical changes in my body, but as a matter of personal experience and personal truth, I find this astonishing. The morning prayer is especially poignant to me, "*Modeh/ah ani* . . . I offer thanks to You,/ever-living Sovereign,/that You have restored my soul to me in mercy:/How great is Your trust."[21] Again, here my wonder acknowledges that this gift of consciousness comes from beyond me and I use the metaphor of God or *chayeh haolamim* to express my gratefulness for this gift, for this kindness, and yes, even caring at awakening each morning. (I am eighty, and while awakening is not to be taken for granted by anyone, it is especially poignant as I get older.)

Another example of being grateful for being alive is when I read in the siddur: *m'chaei hakol b'rachamim rabim* ("who enlivens [gives life] to all with great mercy [a mother's compassion]").[22] I feel gratitude for the kindness of being alive. That gratitude extends to the *chayeh haolamim*, to God, and even more, I use the metaphor that this is God's blessing.

### Human Beings in God's Image

Our tradition teaches that every person is made in the image of God.[23] Adin Steinsaltz writes, "In its profoundest being, the soul of man is part of the Divine and, in this respect, is a manifestation of God in the world." Indeed, "the soul of man, in its depths, may be considered to be a part of God."[24] Abraham Joshua Heschel in one of his early poems writes that people are "heralds of God's face.//Our faces, like bits of God."[25] The implication of this is that having a kinship with God, we may feel God's care directly as an individual and through other people. We turn to those now.

## Personally, as an Individual

A person who is in distress such as anxiety, depression, a threat to their health, or other kind of suffering may feel a moment or more of peace and express that with the metaphor that God is comforting them. We may feel that we are as Steinsaltz says, "a part of God."[26]

## Through Other People

We may feel God's caring presence through the agency of other people who are created in the image of God. God is involved in both the one who does the act of kindness and the one who receives it.

People do the caring act, but the push, the nudge, the inspiration comes from beyond them, and we use the metaphor that God is moving them to care. Therefore we might say that God's caring is transitive. When people feel moved to help others that is God's inspiration in the form of an urge to care.

On a personal level I feel *YHVH*'s commanding presence to seek justice, etc. I feel called, charged, urged, pushed to support justice and feed the hungry, etc., and I feel this deeply.[27] Is that God commanding me? My understanding would be that, yes, it is God. It comes from beyond me and I express that through the metaphor of God.

Debra Robbins interprets the words *azer k'negdo* (a fitting helper) to mean, "to help one another/and act as sacred partners with God./Each of them, each of us, made in God's image, meant to help another."[28]

Arthur Green makes this explicit when he says, "The God I know is a divinity that cannot act or be realized in the human world at all except through human actions."[29]

A well-known story illustrates this. A man caught in a flood finally seeks refuge on the roof of his house. A neighbor in a boat comes by to rescue him but he declines help saying that God will save him. The Coast Guard sends a helicopter, which he waves off saying that God will save him. He dies in the flood and finally confronts God and asks, "Why didn't you save me?" God responds: "Who do you think sent the boat and the helicopter?"

A further illustration may help. There is an organization called God's Love We Deliver. They provide meals for people who are ill and cannot cook for themselves. It got its name from a patient who after receiving a meal said, "You are not just delivering food, you deliver God's love."[30]

This leads us to the recipients of the kindness performed by agents of God. I—and I assume all of us—have been the recipients of kindness. I can use the metaphor that God cares for me, that caring coming to me through the agency of another person. I may not feel God's care at the moment when help comes, but reflecting on the kindness shown me, I can say that it ultimately comes from God and I can express my thanks to God with the metaphor that "God cares for me." It is important to say again that this is a metaphor expressing our understanding and says nothing about God. It is our way of expressing our thanks at being cared for and acknowledging that this help ultimately came from a transcendent source.

To put it in another way, we are all God's *malachim* (angels or messengers). Here, the one who responds to God's commanding presence is aware that he/she is God's representative, God's agent or a *malach* (a messenger acting on behalf of God). I certainly have felt that way. The recipient of that kindness or help might say that the person who was the agent of God's help is an "angel" and they might even say, "You are an angel." In either case God's Presence is sensed by both the provider of help and the recipient. Both use metaphors "angel" or "God's messenger" to express that sense. Again this says nothing about God, who is unknowable; it is a human expression.

Akin to this, is the instance, when many years ago, a man who was out of work, came to me to ask for money to prepare for Pesach. When I gave him what he needed he said, "You will be Elijah at our seder this year." This was his way of telling me that I am an angel and indeed Jewish tradition understands Elijah as an angel, a messenger of God.[31]

## K'dushah *(Holiness)*

There is another side to this caring by people who are representatives of God. The word *kadosh* means separate but also has the connotation for us as being spiritually elevated, closer to God. The person who acts doing a mitzvah is made holy. We say *Baruch atah Adonai, Eloheinu*

*Melech haolam, asher kid'shanu b'mitzvotav* (". . . Who has made us holy with God's commandments"). To put it in other terms, God makes us holy when we respond to God's commanding presence. That brings us to a higher level of spirituality, closer to God's Presence.

Now I realize that these *b'rachot* are only said before acts between God and people, ritual acts. Traditionally, there are no such *b'rachot* for acts such as giving *tzedakah* or visiting the sick.[32] Regardless of whether a *b'rachah* is traditionally said, the mitzvot in which we act as God's agents to visit the sick, give to the poor, etc., make us holy in the sense that they elevate us spiritually and bring us closer to God's Presence. Hearing God's commanding presence to say *Ha-Motzi* or to give *tzedakah* is the same commanding presence. I think it would be appropriate for someone to develop a series of *b'rachot* to be said for mitzvot between *adam v'chavero* (between people). For example before giving *tzedakah* one might say: *Baruch atah Adonai, Eloheinu Melech haolam, asher kid'shanu b'mitzvotav v'tzivanu latayt tzedakah.* ("Praised are You, *Adonai* our God, Sovereign of the universe, who hallows us with mitzvot commanding us to give *tzedakah*.")

## Torah Given in Love

The siddur speaks of God's love of Israel demonstrated by God's giving of Torah.[33] Some Jews believe that God gave both the written and oral Torah at Sinai; others say it was given over the centuries or that it was the product of a human sense of the Divine Presence. Some may think that Torah[34] is more a process than a book or books, but no matter how we came to have it or even what it is, it is depicted as a gift God gave to Israel out of love, which is, of course, caring.

The siddur uses the metaphor Torah given out of God's love for Israel for our sense that Torah is a great gift, that we deeply appreciate how it gives guidance and meaning to our lives. It is metaphor for our feeling that we are cared for because we have a guide for our lives. We realize that some passages of Torah may appear obsolete or of only historical interest, such as the building of the Temple and the sacrifices. Some of them are even morally repugnant by today's standards, such as slavery or the wiping out of current inhabitants of the land, but which were common at that time. Still we have a deep sense of thankfulness that we have Torah in the broadest sense: this millennia-old conversation of how we should live and what gives meaning to our lives. It is a text that we renew with new interpretations and understandings in each generation. This is true even with passages that were previously considered archaic.[35] We have this text that comes out of a sense of God's Presence or at least God's Presence is hovering in the background as we renew it and we are deeply grateful for that kindness. The prayer *Sim Shalom* begins with a plea for both peace and *chased* ("kindness") and continues with God's Presence in giving Torah and our love of kindness. We read, "for with the light of Your face (Your presence) you have given us the Torah of life and a love of kindness."[36]

Arthur Green expands this idea that God gives Torah though God's Presence felt by people. Green quotes Exodus 19:19, "Moses spoke and God responded in a voice." Green then refers to a Talmudic passage (BT *B'rachot* 45a), which says that God responded in the voice of Moses. "This," says Green, "seems to say that the *only* voice heard at Sinai was Moses, sometimes possessed by the divine spirit, God responding from *within* Moses's own voice."[37]

When we receive a gift from someone that shows a great deal of thought and is personally meaningful to us we feel that they love us on some level. And, when we are the recipient of the gift of Torah we react by using the metaphor that God loves us. This is certainly a form of caring. We experience God's kindness through those who spoke and created Torah and those who continue to create it and teach it.

An example from childhood may help explain this. A good parent sets rules and standards for their child to keep them safe and to help them grow into responsible, moral, independent adults. The child may chafe at these rules; but, if there were none, the child might feel that the parent doesn't care enough about them. A child may yearn for their parents' guidance.

Similarly, the rules or mitzvot in Torah to create a safe and just society and help us grow may be felt as, to use the metaphor, God's caring.

### God Redeems Us

In Exodus 2:23–25 and 3:7–8 God hears the suffering of Israel under Egyptian bondage and sets about to rescue them. The siddur makes this one of the major themes of the liturgy.[38] While not saying it explicitly, this redemption is out of care, concern, and love for Israel.

Martin Buber understands these events as well as the events at the sea, as "inner history." The events are experienced with "abiding astonishment," as the redemptive hand of God. All of the natural, political, and military explanations only deepen the astonishment and reinforce the divine origin of the event.[39] We may see it as Maurice Friedman does in his book on Martin Buber. He says, "In his darkest hours man feels the hand of God reaching down to him. If he has 'the incredible courage' to take the hand and let it draw him up out of the darkness, he tastes the essence of redemption."[40] And of course, that hand is a metaphor for the hand of a person who is the agent of God.

Many of those of us who were adults during the Six-Day War felt the same way. We could learn all the military and political facts about it but we experienced it in "abiding astonishment" and some experienced it using the metaphor of "divine redemption." (I was ordained that Sunday and we were relieved and jubilant too.)

Seen from our perspective today, this is one more metaphor for the efforts of Moses and others who acted as God's agents in freeing Israel. Buber reminds us that Moses believed, "in the leadership of the God whose voice he heard."[41] Thus, God caring for the enslaved people is through the agency of people. Moses is chosen to go to Pharaoh with Aaron as his spokesman to demand, on God's behalf, that Pharaoh free the people. Moses clearly understands that he is God's agent. This is a case of historical redemption. Here the people experience their freedom as God's act and use the story of redemption to express that experience.

On an individual level, if *Mitzrayim* (Egypt) is interpreted as "tight places," then redemption can also be a personal matter. In this case a friend, clergy person, or therapist would be God's agent in freeing a person from their own tight places and they might experience it as God's care in freeing them.

The advantage of this understanding is that we can take the biblical account of the events and the Haggadah at face value, participating fully in the seder.[42] As Arthur Green says, "Our soul will only respond to Being with a human face."[43] At the same time we can step back and understand that we are reading an account of how the people directly involved experienced it but now understanding it for ourselves as Moses acting as an agent of God. We use the metaphor of divine redemption.[44]

## 4. Summary/Conclusion

Experiencing God's care isn't easy for many of us—it presents many challenges both intellectual and experiential. Nevertheless we do not want to feel alone in an uncaring world. Some Jews may believe in a cosmic figure who loves them unconditionally, but most of us cannot. In this article, I have provided a number of ways in which we might experience God's care. Some or all may resonate in our lives and others may not. Some may be felt immediately and some only afterwards. Experiencing God's care is a basic form of Jewish spiritual life, and I urge readers to find at least some area on which he/she will feel God's caring presence whether personal or through the kindness of others; through redemption, personal or communal, or through Torah.

None of this is easy but it is certainly worth the effort to be open to experiences of that care. It will be rewarding to direct our attention, awareness, and sensitivities to occasions when we can feel God's care through God's agents.

### Notes

1. Elyse D. Frishman, ed., *Mishkan T'filah* (New York: CCAR, 2007), 36–42.
2. *Mishkan T'filah*, 5.
3. *Mishkan T'filah*, 54.
4. *Mishkan T'filah*, 62.
5. Leonard Kravitz and Kerry M. Olitzky, eds., *Pirke Avot* (New York: URJ Press, 1993), 106, where the editors cite R. Meir.
6. Some people try to pronounce the word by adding vowels. They might say Yahway, or Jehovah, which clearly make no sense. Judaism took the vowels (*hataf-patach, cholom, kamatz*) from the word *Adonai* meaning according to Even Shoshan's dictionary *Milon Chadash* (Jerusalem, 1966), 14, "*Elohim*—God" or "*Adon Haolam*—Lord of the world," and placed them under *YHVH* so that it is pronounced, *Adonai*. In short, when we see *YHVH* we pronounce it *Adonai* so it is a word that is composed of the vowels of one word (*Adonai*) and applied to the consonants *YHVH* as a way to say *YHVH*, which is actually unpronounceable.
7. Abraham Joshua Heschel, *I Asked for Wonder—A Spiritual Anthology*, ed. Samuel H. Dresner (New York, 2008), 25, where Heschel says, "'God is one' or 'Holy, holy, holy is the Lord of Hosts' may be used as metaphors in speaking of God."

8. Edwin Goldberg, Janet Marder, Sheldon Marder, and Leon Morris, eds., *Mishkan HaNefesh—Yom Kippur* (New York: CCAR, 2015), 310.

9. Chaim Stern, ed., *Sha'aray T'shuvah* (New York, 1978), 337.

10. Menachem Nachum, *Sefer Me'or 'Aynayim—The Light of the Eyes*, ed. and trans. Arthur Green (Stanford, 2021), 599.

11. *Mishkan T'filah*, 289.

12. Yoel S., "A Hasidic Matan Torah—The Revelation of the Divine Voice Within," https://www.thetorah.com/article/a-hasidic-matan-torah-the-revelation-of-the-divine-voice-within.

13. Abraham Joshua Heschel, *God in Search of Man* (New York, 1955), 74.

14. Heschel, *God in Search of Man*, 106 (italics are his).

15. Heschel, *God in Search of Man*, 111.

16. Fritz A Rothschild, ed., *Between God and Man: An Interpretation of Judaism from the Writings of Abraham Joshua Heschel* (New York, 1959), 52.

17. *Mishkan T'filah*, 64.

18. *Mishkan T'filah*, 60.

19. Lawrence Hoffman, "Jabberwocky, and the Human Condition: Theology for Non-Theologians," https://scriptions.huc.edu/scriptions/jabberwocky-and-the-human-condition-theology-for-non-theologians.

20. Arthur Green, *Judaism for the World* (New Haven, 2020), 75.

There are two other objections to which I can respond.

Some might object saying: "Adam has his personal truth; I have my personal truth. And my personal truth is that I do not feel God's commanding presence; I might like to feel what Adam feels, but his words, as poetic as they might be, do not have the power to convert his wishes to my . . . reality."

This objection has merit. Since this is a personal truth there is no way of objectively deciding between us. Some people may have experiences leading them to the same personal truth I have, others may not.

The second objection is by Eric Caplan in a review of books by Arthur Green, Jay Michaelson, and Elliot Cosgrove. While he refers to these authors, his criticism of them applies to me as well. He says they "strip God of all power and personality leaving the reader to wonder whether what is called 'God' . . . merits that designation." See Eric Caplan, "All in One? Current Theologies," in *CCAR Journal* (Fall 2012): 214.

My reply is that I don't know what use of the word "God" would satisfy him but it is clear to me that God, *YHVH*, is unknowable and undefinable. I don't know anything about God him/her/itself and I don't think he or anyone else does either. It becomes a matter of the metaphors we use and the fallible concepts we may employ. As soon as we say, "God is . . ." we are wrong. When we do that we are at best mistaken, at worst we are setting up an idol.

21. *Mishkan T'filah*, 24.

22. *Mishkan T'filah*, 246.

23. *Mishkan T'filah*, 40.

24. Adin Steinsaltz, *The Thirteen Petaled Rose* (New York: Basic Books, 2006), 37. I am grateful to Dr. Arnold Katz for leading me to this passage.

25. Abraham Joshua Heschel, "Evenings in the City," in *The Ineffable Name of God: Man* (New York, 2007), 79.

26. Steinsaltz, *Thirteen Petaled Rose*, 37.

27. I use that phrase, which I do not believe I coined, but I cannot find any major thinker who uses it in that way. Franz Rosenzweig refers to this although he may be applying it only to ritual practice. He says that Law (*Gesetrz*) must again become commandment (*Gebot*), which seeks to be transformed into deed at the very moment it is heard. "That is for Rosenzweig, the individual in performing a particular law may come via that performance to hear God's commanding voice, to sense His commanding Presence." Lawrence Kaplan, "Kashrut and Kugel: Franz Rosenzweig's 'The Builders' in *Jewish Review of Books* (Winter 2014). See also Benny Kraut, "The Approach to Jewish Law of Martin Buber and Franz Rosenzweig," in *Tradition: A Journal of Orthodox Jewish Thought* 12, nos. 3–4 (Winter–Spring 1972): 58–59, where it says, "Rosenzweig sees that halacha (*gesetz*) must become a personal command (*gebot*) in which we sense God's commanding presence."

28. Debra J. Robbins, *Opening Your Heart With Psalm 27* (New York, 2019), 63. See also pages 98–99, where she refers to the people who helped following a shooting and are "doing God's work."

29. Arthur Green, *Seek My Face* (Woodstock, VT: Jewish Lights, 2003), 130.

30. www.glwd.org. I am grateful to Steve Weitzman for bringing this organization to my attention.

31. http://www.jewishencyclopedia.com/articles/5634-elijah.

32. Some might say that we should not say any words that might delay giving *tzedakah* and others might say that the act itself is the blessing. Others have different reasons. The Rashba said that mitzvot that are not entirely in the hands of the one performing it have no *b'rachah* before it. Elazar of Worms said that giving *tzedakah* was based on logic and common sense and is performed by non-Jews as well as Jews and therefore does not have a *b'rachah*. Maharsham says that in giving *tzedakah* we only give that which God has entrusted us, but does not really belong to us. https://

judaism.stackexchange.com/questions/109036/why-don't-we-say-a-blessing-before-giving-charity. I am grateful to Rabbi Ellen Lippmann for sharing this reference with me.

33. *Mishkan T'filah*, 62.

34. Torah comes from *yoreh* (a trajectory). It can be understood as a book or books, as a path, a way we should go in our lives, a teaching.

35. Arthur Green, *Judaism for the World* (New Haven, 2020), 33 Here Green says, "Oral Torah is an ongoing, living process. In a certain sense *we are* the Oral Torah." On p. 40 Green reinterprets the *Mishkan,* the Temple as the heart. This is only one instance of contemporary renewal of Torah for our time. He takes this further when he says (p. 76), "The Torah narrative is not simply a collection of tales about our ancestors, but a series of gateways—made-up of words, letters, images, even white spaces in the text—through which we may enter into an interior universe."

36. *Mishkan T'filah*, 334.

37. Green, *Judaism for the World*, 171.

38. *Mishkan T'filah*, 70, 72.

39. Martin Buber, *Moses* (Oxford, 1946), 73–74. I do not use the word "miracle" as Buber does because the Hebrew Bible understands everything as God's doing with no special incursion into natural events as is implied in the modern use of the word. The first meaning of the word *neis*, which is in the second Chanukah blessing, is according to Even Shoshan, *pele* (wonder). Shoshan, *Milon Hadash*, 1013. Although the second meaning is an event outside nature.

40. Maurice Friedman, *Martin Buber: The Life of Dialogue*, 4th ed. (London and New York: Routledge, 2002), 156.

41. Buber, *Moses*, 76.

42. This is nothing new. The Rabbis understood that Torah was read on several levels: *p'shat* (simple plain meaning); *remez* (hinted meaning often referring to allegorical meaning); *d'rash* (inquiring or creative understanding); and *sod* (esoteric/mystical meaning). https://biblicalculture.wordpress.com/2012/12/05/the-four-levels-of-interpretation/. We can experience and understand the Exodus on several levels at the same time.

43. Green, *Judaism for the World*, 80.

44. I am aware that the Haggadah says, "And the Eternal brought us forth from Egypt: not by means of an angel, nor by means of a Seraph, nor by means of a messenger" (*Maxwell House Haggadah* [New Edition], 17), but this is a later interpretation of the biblical text in which there is a partnership between God and Moses and, to a lesser extent, with Aaron.

# Can Spinoza's Pantheism and Kaplan's Naturalism Be Compatible with Buber's Existentialism?

## Three Manifestations of a Universal God

*Rabbi Paul Menitoff*

### Preface

The existentialist Martin Buber (1878–1965), the religious naturalist Mordechai Kaplan (1881–1983), and the pantheist Baruch Spinoza (1632–1677), were three of our people's most radical and prominent Jewish philosophers.[1]

Buber was abandoned by his mother at an early age and was raised in his grandparents' observant home until his teens. He then lived with his secular father, permanently abandoning halachah and adopting a non-literalist perspective regarding Jewish sacred texts and practices. In 1899, Buber married Paula Winkler, a non-Jew. His Jewish life style and his ideologies regarding Jewish nationalism, Israel's future as a binational state, and his existential theology diminished his acceptance in some Jewish academic, Zionist, and religious circles.[2]

Buber explained how mutually caring special relationships can result in I-Thou encounters during which the parties can *experience* the Eternal Thou—God. In contrast, the I-It relationship is the second relational category Buber described: one in which the other is treated as an object. These are utilitarian, for example, with

RABBI PAUL MENITOFF (C70) is the executive vice president emeritus, CCAR. After retiring, he founded Catalyst for Justice with a Black journalist and another community activist; this project attempts to decrease the incidence of inappropriate racial profiling and promote effective community policing by law enforcement agencies in racially diverse Palm Beach County, Florida.

a salesperson or with the clerk at the checkout counter. They are matter-of-fact, civil, encounters. They are necessary and maybe pleasant, but casual relationships. By necessity, most of our daily interactions are I-It experiences. Our relationships with those to whom we are close—for example, our partners, children, and special friends or family members—are relationships in which we can be most open to experiencing I-Thou moments. Perhaps the feeling of love is the nearest description of the I-Thou experience.

Rabbi Mordecai Kaplan was born in Lithuania. When he was eight years old, he and his family moved to the United States. Although his early education was traditional Jewish, later he attended public schools and graduated from Columbia. He received his rabbinic training at the Jewish Theological Seminary. He served as first dean of the Seminary's Teachers Institute and then as a professor of homiletics, midrash, and philosophies of religion at the school.[3]

Kaplan was excommunicated by the Union of Orthodox Rabbis on June 14, 1945, and his Reconstructionist prayer book was burned by some of its members. He was also shunned by many of his colleagues at the Jewish Theological Seminary because of his non-literalist understanding of sacred texts and his description of God as a non-anthropomorphic power.[4] Despite the opposition, Kaplan and his followers founded a dynamic American Jewish movement that spawned the Reconstructionist Rabbinic College, liturgies, and rabbinic and synagogue organizations—each based on Kaplan's theology and vision. Kaplan's ideology has significantly influenced many progressive rabbis and laypeople who are not directly involved in the Reconstructionist Movement.

Kaplan's theology was radical—positing God as a *power*, not a *person*: "God is the Power in the cosmos that gives human life direction that enables human beings to reflect the image of God. That conception of God does not require our believing in miracles, which imply the suspension of natural law."[5] God is "that aspect of the cosmos that makes for salvation." He defines salvation as "self-fulfillment."[6]

Kaplan also urged Jews to think of themselves as not just a religion, but as a peoplehood. "The time has now come for all affirmative Jews to recapture the long-lost experience of oneness with the People of Israel past, present and future. This involves a broadening of the conception of Jewish religion so as to render it compatible with *theological* pluralism."[7] Judaism is "something far more comprehensive than Jewish religion. It includes that nexus of a history, literature, language, social organization, folk sanctions, standards of conduct, social and spiritual ideals, esthetic values, which in their totality form a civilization."[8]

Spinoza's family were prominent members of the Amsterdam Sephardic Jewish community. He studied Hebrew, Bible, and Talmud in a yeshivah. Afterwards, he was attracted to the writings of Maimonides, Gersonides, and the commentaries of Abraham Ibn Ezra—the first two were Aristotelians and all emphasized reason in their philosophies. Spinoza, influenced by the intellectual environment of Amsterdam, studied Latin, mathematics, and the physical sciences. Spinoza was also influenced by the Scholasticism of St. Thomas Aquinas, based on Aristotelian logic, and Descartes's focus on reason rather than tradition. His ideas were viewed as heresy by his Jewish community.[9]

Spinoza's excommunication, at age twenty-three, from his Dutch Jewish community resulted from his pantheism and his disbelief in the divine authorship of the Torah and the Oral law.[10] Unlike Buber's and Kaplan's experiences, Spinoza's excommunication resulted in total ostracism by the Jewish community and rejection by his family. Initially, following his excommunication, most of his friends were Mennonites whose views were akin to the Quakers. He supported himself as an optician and by tutoring students in Latin, Hebrew, and philosophy. He moved ultimately to The Hague where he completed the *Ethics* and lived until his death. He was buried in a church cemetery, but never converted.[11]

Spinoza believed that God/nature is the "only one infinite, unlimited, self-caused Substance (*Deus sive natura*—God or nature). Substance being two aspects of the ultimate unity of existence. Substance possesses a theoretical infinity of attributes, only two of which are apprehended by man: extension (matter) and thought (mind). God or nature can also be viewed as a whole made up of individual finite entities. All of the particular ideas and bodies of the world are defined by Spinoza as 'modes' of the one Substance. God exists in all things as their universal essence; they exist in God as subsidiary modifications."[12] It is inseparable from the workings of all that exists. Nothing can happen that is not in harmony with natural law—God's law, nature. Knowing God results in experiencing peace: that is to say, salvation. The path to peace is studying science.[13]

## The Issue

Mordecai Kaplan's religious naturalism and Baruch Spinoza's pantheism are commonly viewed as being diametrically opposed to Martin Buber's religious existentialist philosophy. Pantheism and naturalism emphasize *humans as being part of nature, functioning in concert with the laws of nature, explicated by the physical, behavioral, and social sciences.* Existentialism—though extremely difficult to define with precision—can be said to focus upon the lived experiences of the individual's thoughts and feelings as the basis for the person's actions. In other words, existentialists trust, more than science and other sources of knowledge, *how they personally process intellectually and emotionally their personal experiences as the basis for their behavior.*

## A Perspective

Each of the three theologies are compelling and believable to me because they are in sync with science and my experiences, and they help me find meaning in my existence. For many years, I therefore tolerated the apparent incompatibility between Buber's existentialism and the pantheism of Spinoza and naturalism of Kaplan.

Gradually, however, I began *viewing their theological perspectives as describing ways we experience* three *separate manifestations of one God*: (1) the laws of nature, (2) God as a power—not as a person, and (3) God's divine presence through sacred relationships and encounters. The first two are grounded in Baruch Spinoza's pantheism and Mordecai Kaplan's religious naturalism, the third in Martin Buber's religious existentialism. This perspective provides me with a coherent Jewish theology.

In addition, the compatibility of their theologies is enhanced by their views of God, which contribute to a sense of meaning in one's life: Spinoza indicates that the more we understand God and the laws of nature, the more we know peace, "intellectual joy," and happiness;[14] Buber indicates that "after an encounter with God, the individual [is] enriched with new meaning."[15] For Kaplan, "God is the Power that makes for salvation [i.e., self-fulfillment]."[16] For each of them, if meaning is to be found in existence, it is to be discovered in this life, since all three reject a belief in a supernatural afterlife. They do not believe in the concept of physical resurrection of the dead when the Messiah arrives nor in the idea of *olam haba* (the world-to-come) that are described in the Talmud and Rabbinic commentaries.

I am *not advocating* that their theologies necessarily be understood by everyone as pointing to separate manifestations of God. *Nor am I urging* readers to accept that their views of God's role in enhancing our sense of meaning in our lives and their rejection of a life after death necessarily make their theologies more compatible. I *am suggesting* a way, for those who, like me, find each of their theologies compelling, to view them as compatible, and to integrate them into a personal theology that is also not inconsistent with science.

### A Personal Example of Integrating Three Jewish Thinkers into a Multidimensional View of God

Influenced by Spinoza's pantheism (*Deus sive natura*, God or nature), I believe we experience one major manifestation of God through the laws of nature. We are each part of a single whole—a Oneness—composed of matter and energy, a power that functions according to a system: God's laws—the laws of nature. God is the Ultimate Power, a totality of all of its parts—including its creations.[17] The laws of nature are, therefore, synonymous with God's laws.[18] Those laws are revealed (revelation) to us through the physical, behavioral, and social sciences—often supported by our own observations and experiences. These laws describe how God, and therefore the world, operates. I am reminded of this manifestation of God regularly when I recite the *Sh'ma*, which affirms God's unity.[19]

I-Thou relationships, described by Buber,[20] help me feel deeply connected to others, to experience personally and emotionally a sacred closeness to the Divine Presence—another manifestation of God. In Buber's terminology, the Eternal Thou, in mine—the Oneness or nature. The Divine Presence I experience in I-Thou encounters are made possible by the Power inherent in nature in accordance with the physical, behavioral, and social sciences.

Experiencing the Divine Presence through sacred relationships with others results in my feeling an *emotional* connectedness to

God. This manifestation of God is especially believable and helpful to me, since humans are "social animals."[21] Experiencing I-Thou encounters lessens my existential sense of aloneness and increases my sense of living a meaningful existence.

For me, Kaplan's description of God as a Power, not a person, points to another manifestation of God. He states it as, "the Power in the cosmos that gives human life direction that enables the human being to reflect the image of God . . . and the Power that makes for salvation[22] ['self-fulfillment']."[23] That Power is the same Power, nature, that we understand through the laws of nature. Furthermore, the Ultimate Power, *Nature*, consumes and directs *all* life (not only human life, as Kaplan posits). According to my perspective, *all creatures* are part of the Oneness of God and, therefore, are both part of God's image through their existence and reflect that image through their behavior.

Kaplan's theological perspective, as does Spinoza's, supports my seeking scientific explanations, rather than appealing to supernatural ones, to understand how the world functions. For example, accepting the scientific theory of evolution, I am confident that humans, plants, and animals evolve, driven by survival and reproductive instincts. As animals and humans evolve, their most successful strategies for survival evolve beyond the fight-flight-conquer pattern to include manipulation-cooperation with others.[24]

In addition, if I heed the laws of nature, informed by scientific guidance, this theological perspective affords me extensive control over my life, including the possibility of improving myself and the world. Some examples: exercise and a proper diet could increase the probabilities of my living a healthier and, perhaps, longer life. Also, if enough of us protect our planet's ecology, we could reasonably expect to prolong our planet's existence. COVID-19 is caused by a virus, not divine punishment. It is likely that the virus will be contained and ultimately conquered by scientists continuing to use their knowledge of the laws of nature, as they did to develop vaccines—a scientific "miracle," not a biblical style one.

Kaplan's views regarding Jewish peoplehood echoes for me Buber's views that relationships provide meaning in our lives. In this case, the individual Jew is in a relationship with a group[25]— the Jewish people.[26] Influenced by Kaplan, I view Jewish rituals, symbols, holiday observances, and liturgy as habitual "triggers" reminding me that I am reflecting the observances of multitudes of Jews throughout time: past, present, and future. These acts of consciously transferring sacredness into my life strengthen my relationship with our people—making me feel "bigger than life." It adds meaning to my existence. It symbolizes who I am, where I came from, and, in some sense, extends my existence, the existence of my people and my people's values beyond my own lifetime. They cause me to pause, appreciate, sanctify, and recall my relationships with the Divine Presence, my family, close friends, and the Jewish people—their narratives, highest values, and teachings— and often to experience the Eternal Thou. These values, practices, and narratives bind Jews together in a group—the Jewish people. Our peoplehood—civilization—is of paramount importance to Kaplan and is also an essential component of my Judaism.

Viewing God through the lens of the laws of nature discourages me from adopting unrealistic expectations and avoiding my responsibilities. I am not controlled by the whims of a supernatural God. There is some consistency built into the laws of nature. God does not suspend those laws in order to respond to my personal needs. God does not miraculously heal a disease for which scientists have not yet discovered a cure or alter the natural law that death is a fact of life.

## Concluding Thoughts

I have suggested in this article that the theologies of three radical Jewish thinkers, two naturalists and one existentialist, can be viewed, not as contradictory, but instead as describing manifestations of one God: a God whose manifestations may provide emotional and intellectual supports for providing meaning in our lives.[27]

For me, these three manifestations of one God, as pointed to by Spinoza, Buber, and Kaplan, are together, a compelling, believable, and compatible theology. The manifestations provide paths to finding meaning that is not contrary to the laws of nature or science. Buber taught that experiencing *the Divine Presence through special relationships* brings the *sacred* into our lives and *lessens our existential aloneness*. Spinoza believed the more we know about God, and understand we are all a part of nature and ruled by its laws, the more we will experience *peace*. Kaplan indicated that God is the Power that guides humans to live so we reflect God's image and enables us to experience *"self-fulfillment"—"making the most of human life."*[28] Experiencing sacredness, peace, fulfillment, and connectedness provides me with a reassuring sense that my life matters.[29]

## Notes

1. Perhaps my perspective will be helpful to progressive rabbis, other clergy, and lay readers. Readers may find the following publications useful: *Finding God: Ten Jewish Responses* by Rifat Sonsino and Daniel B. Syme (URJ, 1986) provides a concise overview of Spinoza's, Buber's, Kaplan's, and other's theologies. *God in Our Relationships*, by Dennis Ross (Jewish Lights, 2003) is an accessible description of Buber's I-Thou and I-It relationships along with many examples. Dennis Ross, *A Year with Martin Buber: Wisdom on the Weekly Torah Portions* (Philadelphia: Jewish Publication Society, 2021) illustrates interpretive applications of Buber's philosophy. In addition, *Martin Buber: A Life of Faith and Dissent*, by Paul Mendes-Flohr (Yale Press, 2019) describes Buber's life and philosophy. *The Spinoza Problem*, by Irvin D. Yalom (Basic Books, 2012) is a novel that provides insights into Spinoza's life and philosophy. *Judaism Without Supernaturalism*, by Mordecai Kaplan (Reconstructionist Press, 1967) succinctly describes Kaplan's philosophy. See also Mordecai Kaplan's *Judaism as a Civilization* (Macmillan Publishing Company,1934). *Jewish People, Jewish Thought*, by Robert M. Seltzer (Macmillan Publishing Company, 1980) describes the positions of each of these thinkers and others within a historical context. Michael Marmur and David Ellenson in *American Jewish Thought Since 1934* (Brandeis University Press, 2020) presents background information and selected texts from modern thinkers, including Mordecai Kaplan. Martin Buber, *I and Thou* (A Scribner Classic, Collier Books, Macmillan Publishing Company, 1987).

2. Paul Mendes-Flohr, Martin Buber: A Life of Faith and Dissent (New Haven and London: Yale University Press, 2019), 1–14.

3. Robert M. Seltzer, Jewish People, Jewish Thought (New York: Macmillan Publishing Company, 1980), 748–49.

4. Zachary Silver, "The Excommunication of Mordecai Kaplan," https://www.academia.edu/7293900/The_Excommunication_of_Mordecai_Kaplan, 1–28.

5. Mordecai M. Kaplan, Judaism Without Supernaturalism (New York: Reconstructionist Press, 1967), 112.

6. Kaplan, Judaism Without Supernaturalism, 119.

7. Kaplan, Judaism Without Supernaturalism, 239.

8. Mordecai Kaplan, Judaism as a Civilization: Toward a Reconstruction of American Jewish Life (New York: Schocken Books, 1967), 178, 173–85 (useful comments regarding civilization),

515–22 (Kaplan describes his proposed program for reconstructing American Jewish Life).

9. Isidore Singer, ed., The Jewish Encyclopedia (New York: Ktav Publishing), vol. 11, 511–12.

10. Steven Nadler, "Spinoza: Who Wrote the Bible Determines How We Read It" (2020), https:/thetorah.co/article/spinoza-who-wrote-the-bible-determines-how-we-read-it.

11. Singer, ed., Jewish Encyclopedia, vol. 11, 512–13.

12. Seltzer, Jewish People, Jewish Thought, 553–55.

13. Seltzer, Jewish People, Jewish Thought, 552, 556.

14. Seltzer, Jewish People, Jewish Thought, 745.

15. Seltzer, Jewish People, Jewish Thought, 751.

16. Kaplan, Judaism Without Supernaturalism, 110.

17. Rifat Sonsino and Daniel B. Syme, Finding God: Ten Jewish Responses (New York: Union of American Hebrew Congregations, 1986), 81–82, 78–85 provides a succinct discussion of Spinoza's views, as does 85–95 of Buber's, and 105–17 of Kaplan's.

18. Walter Isaacson, Einstein (New York: Simon and Schuster, 2007), 334–35, 387–89. Einstein identified as a Jew and sympathetic to Spinoza's pantheistic views.

19. Deut. 6:4.

20. Martin Buber, I and Thou (New York: A Scribner Classic, Collier Books, Macmillan Publishing Company, 1987), 1–18, 121–37.

21. This concept was first advanced by Aristotle and has been well established ever since by behavioral science research and is frequently discussed in popular forums. For example, the magazine Psychology Today, on July 20, 2015, posted "What Do We Need to Survive," by Samantha Boardman, pointing out that in Abraham Maslow's "hierarchy of needs," love and belonging are in third position following physiological and safety needs. As recently as May 17, 2019, New York Times columnist David Brooks wrote in his op-ed column that Columbia University Professor Martha Welch, who researches early developmental needs, indicated that human emotional health relies on "connection with others." The Social Animal by Elliot Aronson (1972, since then eleven editions) provides extensive behavioral science information. A summary of the eleventh edition is available on thepowermoves.com.

22. Kaplan's definition of salvation is, of course, different from some Christian views of salvation based on the concept of "Original Sin" from which people must be saved.

23. Kaplan, Judaism Without Supernaturalism, 110, 112, 119.

24. Kaplan, Judaism Without Supernaturalism, 114.

25. Buber's relationship concepts, as I interpret them, can be logically extended to describe how people relate to groups. An explanation is, however, beyond the scope of this article.

26. Michael Marmur and David Ellenson, American Jewish Thought Since 1934 (Waltham, MA: Brandeis University Press, 2020) 263–67.

27. Based on my experience, I am convinced it is important that rabbis frequently share with their congregants their beliefs about God, the implications of those beliefs and how those beliefs may be helpful to them in finding meaning in their lives. Most highly educated Jews are not highly educated in Judaism. It is, therefore, essential that rabbis do not assume that their congregants understand that the human characteristics rabbis sometimes attribute to God or language used by some rabbis that seem to imply divine authorship of some sacred texts is metaphoric. If rabbis are not clear, they risk that neither they nor Judaism will be taken seriously by modern Jews.

28. Kaplan, Judaism Without Supernaturalism, 111–15.

29. My theological perspective, my thoughts and feelings regarding Judaism, the Jewish people and Jewish life, some described in this article, have been significantly influenced by the following individuals: Michael Barenbaum, Eugene Borowitz, Martin Buber, Gustav Buchdahl, Phil and Anne Gaines, Roland Gittelsohn, Mordechai Kaplan, Richard Levy, Bernard Mehlman, Albert and Lillian Menitoff, Rita Menitoff, Michael Meyer, Alvin Reines, Stanley Ringler, James Rosenberg, Alvin Roth, Rifat Sonsino, Baruch Spinoza, and Samuel Wolk.

# Isaac and Iphigenia

*Rabbi Elaine Rose Glickman*

### Introduction: The Near-Sacrifice of Isaac and Iphigenia

A deity demands the sacrifice of a father's most precious child. Without sharing the prophecy with the child's mother, the father lures the child to the place of sacrifice by inviting them to participate in a sacred ritual. As the moment of sacrifice approaches, the child is saved by the sudden appearance of an animal to be slaughtered in their stead. Although the child never again speaks to their father, they continue to worship faithfully the god who ordered the sacrifice.

Is it the hallowed narrative of *Akeidat Yitzhak*? Or the Greek myth of Iphigenia at Aulis?

The answer is yes.

Abraham's binding and near-sacrifice of his favored son, Isaac, recounted in Genesis 22:1–19, is familiar to us. The ordeal of the Mycenean princess Iphigenia at the ancient port of Aulis may be less so. Here is the story of Iphigenia:[1]

As the united forces of ancient Greece—over a thousand ships, led by Iphigenia's father Agamemnon—gather at Aulis to cross the Aegean Sea and prepare for the Trojan War,[2] favorable winds inexplicably cease. The mighty army stalls on the shore, unable to continue the journey towards Troy. Inquiring why the winds have been withheld, the seer Calchas learns—and reveals to Agamemnon —that the goddess Artemis[3] demands the sacrifice of Iphigenia. After initially resisting Calchas's prophecy, Agamemnon lures her to Aulis by telling her mother Clytemnestra that Iphigenia is to marry the great Myrmidon warrior Achilles.

After arriving at Aulis, Iphigenia discovers the ruse and learns that she has been summoned not to be married but to be sacrificed.

RABBI ELAINE ROSE GLICKMAN (C98) is an author and the editor-in-chief of the *CCAR Journal: The Reform Jewish Quarterly*.

Clytemnestra never wavers in her fierce and increasingly desperate opposition to Agamemnon's plan, but Iphigenia comes to accept and even embrace her fate. As Calchas holds the knife over her, however, Iphigenia vanishes—replaced by a deer sacrificed in her stead. Iphigenia is spirited away to Tauris, where she serves as a priestess to Artemis, the goddess who called for her death.

## The Similarities

The obvious similarities in the trials of Isaac and Iphigenia are immediate and startling. Delving deeper into the narratives, however, yields further and perhaps even more intriguing parallels between the stories:

**The reaction of the fathers**. Neither Abraham nor Agamemnon reveals the planned sacrifice to their children's mothers. Agamemnon constructs an elaborate charade to deceive his wife, such a scheme being necessary in order to lure Iphigenia to Aulis. Abraham, who enjoys easy access to his son, maintains secrecy simply by spiriting Isaac away in the early morning hours.[4] Although Abraham and Agamemnon appear cold and determined in their obedience and actions, both also display emotional anguish and endeavor to circumvent the divine decree.[5]

**The presence of young men**. Both Isaac and Iphigenia are accompanied by young men on the way to the place of sacrifice. Iphigenia's escorts are officers charged with keeping her safe until she can be sacrificed and preventing her escape; as Isaac is a young man and likely more vigorous than his father, the servants whom Abraham brings may fill a similar need. Although Isaac's young men do not attend the (aborted) sacrifice, they do see Abraham return alone; and while several versions of the myth have Iphigenia's officers separated from her at the moment of sacrifice, they are able to observe the bloodied altar and to surmise (incorrectly) that the blood is that of Iphigenia. Therefore—as we will discuss below—the young men may have been intended not only to ensure but also to testify that the sacrifice was completed.

**The fathers' hints to the children**. Well before the children can guess their fathers' plans to sacrifice them, Abraham and

Agamemnon speak obliquely of what is to befall Isaac and Iphigenia. When Isaac asks why he and his father are venturing toward the place of sacrifice with wood and firestone—but no animal—Abraham answers, "God will see to the [sacrifice], my son."[6] Iphigenia expresses a wish to sail to Troy with her beloved father, to which Agamemnon responds, "[T]here is yet a sailing for you . . . alone, apart from your father."[7]

**The reaction of the children**. While the Book of Genesis and the basic version of the Iphigenia myth grant little if any agency to the children, later writers ascribe to them initial resistance, followed by eloquent acceptance of their lot. Upon Isaac's realizing the implication of Abraham's not bringing an animal for sacrifice, "fear and dread fell upon Isaac." This sentiment, however, gives way not only to resignation but to resolve that the ritual be performed properly: "Bind my hands and my feet," Isaac cautions his father. "When I see the knife coming at me, I may flinch involuntarily and thus disqualify myself as an offering."[8] Iphigenia first pleads with Agamemnon: "Slay me not before my time, for sweet it is to behold the light"[9]—but soon acquiesces to her sacrifice: "I have determined to die, and this I would fain do gloriously, I mean, by dismissing all ignoble thoughts."[10]

The bond between mother and child—ignored in the Book of Genesis and the original Iphigenia story—is also amplified in these commentaries. According to Rabbinic literature, Isaac's last words are a plea to Abraham not to "tell Mother about this while she is standing over a pit or on a rooftop, for she might throw herself down and be killed."[11] Euripides assigns similar sentiments to Iphigenia, who parts from her devastated mother by begging, "Cease [weeping] . . . obey me in this. Neither . . . cut off the locks of thine hair nor put on black garments . . . [T]hou wilt be glorious."[12]

**The substitution of an animal**. The climax of both stories is, of course, the miraculous appearance of an animal to be slaughtered in the children's stead—a ram for Isaac and a deer for Iphigenia. While Jewish tradition often cites *Akeidat Yitzhak* as evidence for the singular Israelite rejection of human sacrifice, the parallel in the Iphigenia story[13] suggests that this trope—and this rejection—are not unique to our ancestors.

Rather, this anecdotal substitution of animal sacrifice in place of human sacrifice appears to reflect both Israelite and Greek practice. In the Book of Exodus, for example, God commands: "Every first issue of the womb is Mine . . . you must redeem every first-born among your sons,"[14] a tradition maintained for centuries through animal sacrifice, consecration to temple service, and the ritual of *pidyon haben*. And despite abundant Greek myths relating tales of human sacrifice,[15] scholars Robert Graves and Raphael Patai hold that "the Greeks . . . had acquired a horror of human sacrifice at about the same period as the Hebrews."[16]

**The "reward" for obedience**. Both Abraham and Agamemnon appear to be rewarded for their willingness to sacrifice their children; God promises Abraham that he will father numerous children and that nations will be blessed through his descendants,[17] and Agamemnon receives the winds necessary for his forces to advance upon—and eventually annihilate—the kingdom of Troy. Yet this formula of obedience and reward is not so straightforward, for these "rewards" have already been pledged and foretold—for Abraham, in numerous passages in the Book of Genesis;[18] and for Agamemnon, in Queen Hecuba's dream of a flaming torch, understood by the seer Aesacus to mean that her son Paris would bring ruin to Troy, and Zeus's previous portent that the Greeks would conquer Troy after nine years.

**The disappearance of the child**. Despite the wondrous survival of the children, both Isaac and Iphigenia remain hidden and might well be presumed dead. The Book of Genesis states explicitly that "Abraham then returned to his servants . . . and Abraham stayed in Beersheva."[19] Saved from sacrifice, Iphigenia is immediately and secretly taken to labor in the temple of Diana in Tauris.[20]

There may be a reason that the spared children do not return to their former lives: The failure of their fathers to complete the sacrifices might have been seen not as a glorious miracle but as a negligence of duty. Ancient narratives suggest that the sacrifice of a child ensured relief from famine or victory in battle;[21] perhaps Abraham's servants were meant to witness that he had done what was necessary to guarantee his emerging nation prosperity and success, and the reappearance of Isaac would have shattered confidence in and loyalty to Abraham. Many versions of the Iphigenia myth—though, interestingly, not Euripides's tragedy—similarly envision the substitution of an animal as a clandestine act, perhaps recognized not even by Calchas, the seer charged with performing the sacrifice. Assured that Iphigenia's death would assuage Artemis's fury over Agamemnon's killing of a deer and hasten the Greeks' conquest of Troy, Agamemnon's men might have felt anger and fear—rather than relief and awe—had she returned alive from the place of sacrifice.

**The estrangement of child from family**. Long after belief in the completed sacrifices might have proved strategically important—and seemingly at odds with later interpretive traditions that cast Isaac and Iphigenia as willing participants—the children's estrangement from their families of origin persists.[22] While Isaac does eventually settle in the same region of the Negev as Abraham, he does not do so until after Sarah's death, and he never again speaks to his father. Iphigenia, serving Diana at the shrine in Tauris, fails to recognize and is not recognized by her beloved brother Orestes when he arrives on the peninsula.

**Continued service to the god**. Despite the rift between the children and their families, Isaac and Iphigenia remain devoted to the deities who commanded their sacrifice. Rabbinic tradition holds that immediately after his life was spared, Isaac went to study God's law;[23] and the Book of Genesis recounts his fidelity to God and his acquiescence to God's plans for him and his descendants. And although the hardships of her life in Tauris will come to sour Iphigenia on the worship of Diana, she charges the Greeks before her (ostensible) death: "Raise aloft the paen . . . [celebrate] Diana . . . and let the joyful strain go forth . . . Encircle [with dances] around the temple and the altar Diana, queen Diana, the blessed."[24] While on one level this continued allegiance serves a practical purpose for the children—they lack the resources to develop an independent and self-sufficient life—on another level it attests to the eternal and indisputable power of the gods over their followers.

## The Differences

**The use of an intermediary**. In the Book of Genesis, God commands Abraham directly regarding the sacrifice of Isaac; Abraham also intends to perform his son's sacrifice and is the one to slaughter the ram in Isaac's stead. The Iphigenia myth, however, assigns these tasks to Calchas; as the seer among the Greeks, he hears, interprets, and carries out the will of the gods. This contrast underscores a major difference in the Hebrew and Greek theological systems; whereas the former envisages a deity who communicates with and works through "ordinary" people, the latter establishes a hierarchy in which the gods are concerned almost solely with nobles, restricting their revelations and direct involvement to a select few.

**The place of the mother**. Despite playing an active and essential part in the earlier narratives of Genesis, Abraham's wife and Isaac's mother Sarah is completely absent from this climactic tale of the *Akeidah*. Even later commentaries assign her a minimal and passive role in the story and its outcome. With the expansion of the myth of Iphigenia, however, comes a correspondingly expanded presence for her mother Clytemnestra. Agamemnon is dismayed but not entirely surprised that she accompanies Iphigenia to Aulis, and Clytemnestra quickly enmeshes herself in the action surrounding her husband and daughter—delivering to Agamemnon a blistering charge of his previous crimes against her, conspiring with Achilles to foil the sacrifice, joining with Iphigenia in lamenting her fate, and (eventually) taking revenge by killing her husband. While sexism and the marginalization of women were at least as much a part of Greek as Hebrew culture, the presence of strong and active goddesses in the pantheon of Greek deities may have allowed and even encouraged the elaboration of female characters as myths developed.

**The reason for the sacrifice**. Isaac and Iphigenia are to be sacrificed for very different reasons. The Book of Genesis introduces *Akeidat Yitzhak* by stating simply that "God tested Abraham,"[25] and the sacrifice is aborted once Abraham convinces God of his reverence for the Divine.[26] According to the Iphigenia myth, her death will satisfy Artemis's rage at Agamemnon for slaying a deer—and, therefore, bring the winds needed for the Greeks to advance upon and defeat Troy.

For all of its cruelty, the order for Iphigenia's sacrifice possesses a rationale that seems to be lacking in the Isaac narrative. Among the main reasons for human sacrifice—whether in theory or in practice—is to guarantee success in war. The other prominent stories of human sacrifice in the Bible, in fact, are explicitly associated with combat; in the Book of Judges, Jephthah sacrifices his daughter after prevailing over the Ammonites,[27] and in the second book of Kings, the ruler of Moab sacrifices his firstborn son during a battle with the Israelites.[28] Despite the Hebrew Bible's ostensible abhorrence of human sacrifice, both of these acts appear efficacious; Jephthah's slaughter of his child goes unpunished, and God turns the divine wrath on the Israelites after the Moabite king's sacrifice.[29]

And the context as well as a brief passage in the *Akeidat Yitzhak* narrative suggest that this story of sacrifice may also have its roots in conflict. Immediately before *Akeidat Yitzhak* is the conclusion of a pact between Abraham and Avimelech, the mighty king whom Abraham had feared might kill him, and Avimelech's implicit acknowledgment of Abraham's greater power;[30] in the context of ancient Levantine practices, Abraham may have felt compelled to sacrifice his son to show gratitude for God's favor and to ensure continued victories. This possibility is strengthened by what might otherwise seem an irrelevant phrase in the blessing Abraham receives after demonstrating his willingness to sacrifice Isaac; amid the promises of numerous descendants and universal acclaim—echoes of vows God has already made to Abraham—God offers a new prophesy related to military triumph: "Your descendants shall seize the gates of their foes."[31] Rather than a random intrusion into the narrative, these words hint that the origins and significance of *Akeidat Yitzhak* are linked to the practice of human sacrifice in relation to war.[32]

**The fate of the actors**. Perhaps the greatest difference between the stories of Isaac and Iphigenia lies in the destinies of their characters. Whether motivated by fealty to God or desire for victory in battle, Abraham is requited for his willingness to sacrifice Isaac; he becomes a great nation with numerous descendants and influence among the peoples of the world. Even the death of his wife Sarah is eased by his subsequent marriage to Keturah and the birth of six more children.[33] Isaac, too, enjoys marriage, wealth, descendants, the high regard of the still-mighty Avimelech, and divine sustenance and protection.[34] The players in the Iphigenia myth are not nearly as fortunate; spared from slaughter, Iphigenia for years labors miserably in the temple of Diana at Tauris, and—despite his soldiers' triumph at Troy—Agamemnon is killed by Clytemnestra upon returning home. Abraham and Isaac appear no more meritorious than Agamemnon and Iphigenia; rather, the contrast in their fates underscores a moralistic Hebrew theology that prioritizes and promises reward for piety and obedience, and a Greek value system that envisions little if any link between virtue and success.

## Conclusion

Examining Torahitic narratives and laws with reference to those of other civilizations is not a new or original pursuit. However, such work tends to emphasize commonalities between the Hebrews and other Near Eastern cultures—the Sumerians, Hittites, Akkadians, and Babylonians—and perhaps fails to recognize fully the presence and influence of our Aegean neighbors.

Our most documented contacts with Greece obviously occurred after Alexander the Great's 333–332 BCE conquest of the Levant, and we acknowledge Greek impact on naming, synagogue adornments, and the like. However, the relationship between Hebrew and Greek culture of that era is cast as primarily one of hostility; tales of the morally superior Hebrews fighting off debauched pagans, and the Greeks corrupting sacred Hebrew scriptures with the Septuagint, depict Greece as a negative influence at best and—at worst—an existential threat to the Hebrew establishment.

However, scholars attest to mingling between ancient Hebrews and Greeks centuries earlier—during the period that the myths of the Torah arose.[35] This establishment of physical and chronological proximity suggests a Greek presence as the basic elements of our culture were being developed—including our most hallowed narratives and values—and a process of imparting, sharing, and blending very different than that seen in the post-Alexander period. This revelation renders all the more intriguing the substantial similarities in Hebrew and Greek myths—the Isaac and Iphigenia stories are only the beginning—and offers fresh and exciting possibilities for understanding our foundational stories and the values they express.[36]

In addition to illuminating our own myths, an understanding of Greek mythology and its development may provide insight into

Rabbinic literature, specifically aggadah. The embellishment of the Isaac story in the midrash and the Iphigenia myth in the plays of Euripides demonstrate striking similarities in how the Hebrews and Greeks used their myths—and, perhaps, how they kept these ancient stories alive and relevant. In writing *Iphigenia at Aulis* and *Iphigenia in Tauris*, Euripides followed the Greek tradition of composing tragedies, using a process very similar to that of our Sages; he selected a well-known myth but amplified it in a way that demonstrated innovation and contained a message—and employed a familiar narrative and figures to speak to his day's events and concerns. While the Iphigenia myth might well have been maintained among the Greeks had *Iphigenia at Aulis* never been written, Euripides's "midrash" infused it with new life and new meaning for new generations—much as our own Rabbis of antiquity interpreted and adapted our foundational texts to fit the needs of their time.

When we acknowledge the parallels not only between Hebrew and Greek myths—but also between the ways in which those myths were preserved and elaborated—we may find a path towards renewed regard and appreciation for our Aegean contemporaries.[37]

## Notes

1. Several versions of this myth have been preserved. The version that follows is not only the most relevant for comparison to *Akeidat Yitzhak* but is also supported by the *Cypria* and *Biblioteca of Pseudo-Apollodorus,* and served as a source for Euripides's tragedies *Iphigenia at Aulis* (405 BCE) and *Iphigenia in Tauris* (413 BCE).

2. The search for kernels of historical truth in mythological accounts of the Trojan War may evoke comparisons to similar efforts on behalf of biblical narratives. Although the Trojan War was understood by ancient Greeks as a historical event, it was widely dismissed as a mere myth preserved most notably by the Homerian epics of the late eighth to early seventh centuries BCE. Late-nineteenth-century excavations by German archaeologist Heinrich Schliemann, however, revealed evidence of a horrendous siege near the purported site of ancient Troy in the twelfth century BCE. While these excavations certainly do not give credence to the entire body of Trojan War mythology, they do imply that the story may contain an element of historical truth—much as excavations at Tel Hazor suggest a historical basis for biblical stories of the conquest under Joshua.

3. The names of Artemis and Diana are used interchangeably for the goddesses in the myth, and in this paper.

4. Gen. 22:3. Although Rabbinic literature relates that Abraham mulled confiding in Sarah about God's command and told her that he planned to take Isaac to learn about his Creator, these acts were not necessary for him to secure his son; indeed, the same midrash states that he left early the next morning lest Sarah change her mind overnight and withdraw permission for the journey. Hayim Nahman Bialik and Yehoshua Hana Ravnitsky, *Sefer Ha-Aggadah/The Book of Legends*, trans. William G. Braude (New York: Schocken Books, 1992), text 45, p. 40.

5. For Abraham: Rabbinic commentary renders Abraham a more ambivalent and sympathetic figure; see his dialogue with God based on Gen. 22:2 that might be understood as Abraham's "playing dumb" with regard to whom he was to sacrifice and Abraham's objection that such a sacrifice could not take place without a priest. *B'reishit Rabbah* 55:7. For Agamemnon: Several versions of the myth recount his attempt to send a second message to Clytemnestra instructing her not to bring Iphigenia to Aulis; the plan is foiled when Menelaus intercepts the message.

6. Gen. 22:7–8.

7. Euripides, *Iphigenia at Aulis*, in *The Tragedies of Euripides*, vol. 1, trans. Theodore Alois Buckley (New York: Harper and Brothers, 1892), 272–73.

8. Bialik and Ravnitsky, *Sefer Ha-Aggadah*, text 45, p. 41.

9. Euripides, *Iphigenia at Aulis*, 282–83.

10. Euripides, *Iphigenia at Aulis*, 286.

11. Bialik and Ravnitsky, *Sefer Ha-Aggadah*, text 45, p. 41. In light of the Rabbinic tradition linking *Akeidat Yitzhak* with the death of Sarah, Isaac's concern seems well-founded.

12. Euripides, *Iphigenia at Aulis*, 288.

13. The Greek myth of Phrixus is another, perhaps even more compelling account of an attempted child sacrifice foiled by a ram. In one version of the myth, as Athamas clasps the knife to slay his son Phrixus, a messenger cries out that Zeus abhors human sacrifice; a ram sent by Zeus then rescues Phrixus and carries him to safety. In a neat parallel to the traditions that the ram sacrificed in Isaac's stead had been placed in the thicket by God before the first Shabbat and that it gave rise to the strings of David's harp and the shofar sounded at the Revelation at Sinai, the ram that rescued Phrixus was of divine origin and became the source of the Golden Fleece.

14. Exod. 12:19–20.

15. Including, ironically, the continued saga of Iphigenia, who in her new capacity as a priestess of Artemis will preside over human sacrifices to the goddess.

16. Robert Graves and Raphael Patai, *Hebrew Myths: The Book of Genesis* (New York: Greenwich House, 1983), 177.

17. Gen. 22:16–18.

18. Beginning in Gen. 12:2–3.

19. Gen. 22:19—that is, not "Abraham and Isaac returned . . . ."

20. Euripides, *Iphigenia in Tauris*, 298ff.

21. Graves and Patai, *Hebrew Myths*, 175ff.

22. "Do the will of your Maker," Isaac urges his father (Bialik and Ravnitsky, *Sefer Ha-Aggadah*, text 45, p. 41), while Iphigenia consoles her mother, "Let my father serve the altar with his right hand" (Euripides, *Iphigenia at Aulis*, 289).

23. *Targum Yonatan* on Genesis 22.

24. Euripides, *Iphigenia at Aulis*, 288–89.

25. Gen. 22:1.

26. Gen. 22:12.

27. Judges 11:20ff.

28. II Kings 3:27.

29. Human sacrifice actually seems more palatable in ancient Hebrew than in classical Greek tradition, as powerfully illustrated by the story of Idomeneus. Sailing home from the Trojan War, Idomeneus encounters rough seas and fears for his life; in an obvious parallel to the Jephthah story, he promises Poseidon to sacrifice the first creature he sees upon safely returning home. This unfortunate creature is Idomeneus's son. Unlike God—Who seems to accept the sacrifice of Jephthah's daughter—Poseidon reacts to Idomeneus's deed with rage and unleashes a plague upon Crete as punishment.

30. Gen. 21:22ff.

31. Gen. 22:17b.

32. There are, of course, scholars of biblical criticism who hold that *Akeidat Yitzhak* comprises at least two traditions, one in which Abraham completes the sacrifice and is rewarded for doing so. And the efficacy of human sacrifice—whether completed or attempted—is acknowledged even centuries later; for example, medieval *piyyutim* that charge God to remember the *Akeidah* when judging the Jewish people assume that Abraham's willingness to engage in human sacrifice was pleasing to God. See, among others, Shalom Spiegel, *The Last Trial* (Woodstock, VT: Jewish Lights Publishing, 1993).

33. Gen. 25:1–2.

34. Gen. 25:19–26:33.

35. Graves and Patai, *Hebrew Myths*. Perhaps the most intriguing examples are the revelation that ancient Achaens founded colonies

in the Levant (p. 180) and a daring, convincing identification of the "Hivites" in the Dinah story with Achaen immigrants (p. 240).

36. For example, compare: Genesis 2's account of Eve and the Tree of Knowledge with the myth of Pandora, the first woman, and Pandora's box; God's sorrow at the wickedness and evil of humanity before the biblical Flood story in Genesis 6 with Zeus's rage at the warlike, violent nature of the men he himself had created preceding the Greek myth of a great Flood; Jacob's success with Lavan's sheep in Genesis 30 with the myth of Autolycus; and—perhaps—the parallel between the twelve Olympians and the twelve sons of Jacob. Anticipating discomfort with these (perhaps) purposely overlooked similarities, Graves and Patai note that the Book of Genesis "is far more closely linked with Greek . . . myth than most pious Jews and Christians care to admit" and that some of the most obvious differences between the Hebrew and Greek myths reflect not a unique origin for the stories of Genesis but the fact that Genesis was "edited and re-edited . . . for moralistic ends." Graves and Patai, *Hebrew Myths*, 14.

37. While Hebrew myths are widely treated as more authoritative and historical than their Greek counterparts, Graves and Patai convincingly attribute this to Christianity's preference for their themes and values rather than to any intrinsic superiority. "[T]he Hebrew myths, borrowed by the Christians, gave subject people an equal right to salvation," while "the Olympians [were] banished . . . [P]atriarchal and monotheistic Hebrew myth . . . firmly established the ethical principles of Western [i.e., Christian] life." Graves and Patai, *Hebrew Myths*, 19.

# Book Reviews

*Plunder: A Memoir of Family Property and Nazi Treasure*
by Menachem Kaiser
(Boston and New York: Houghton Mifflin Harcourt, 2021), 277 pp.

The link between ancestry and identity is often explored through media today—from television shows about the genetic ancestry of celebrities to websites that can help one create a family tree to books such as *Inheritance*, a memoir about how a genetic test revealed an unknown aspect of the author's identity.[1] Similarly, *Plunder* by Menachem Kaiser is a story about ancestry; but instead of ancestry being traced through genetics, Kaiser's ancestry and identity are traced through his attempt to reclaim his family's property in Poland.

The title might lead one to expect that *Plunder: A Memoir of Family Property and Nazi Treasure* would fall into the established genre of a family Holocaust memoir. However, Kaiser's journey leads him to encounter unexpected subjects such as Nazi treasure hunters, the cumbersome Polish court system, World War II hobbyists, and conspiracy theorists—keeping the reader surprised and intrigued as Kaiser artfully narrates the multilayered story.

As Kaiser seeks to reclaim an apartment building his grandfather's family owned prior to World War II, he grapples with the meaning of place and history, as to whether something material like a building can or should represent history and/or tradition. This theme is initially developed through Kaiser's trip to the Polish town of Sosnowiec, the location of the family's formerly owned building. Whereas Kaiser views the town and his family's building through the tragic history of World War II, Hanna, a resident of the town, emotes heartwarming affection for Sosnowiec, "in a way that a learned, earned love of a place always is" (p. 45), juxtaposing Kaiser's family's negative perception of the town with the present generation who are removed from it. Through Kaiser's trips to Poland, the reader learns about the region of Silesia, a region that lies in the basin of the Oder River, which begins in the Czech Republic and flows north-northwest through Poland and partially marks the Polish-German border. Within the center of Silesia is a "culture of mystery," a geographical area called Project Riese, a series of seven underground complexes in the Owl mountains, developed through the work of Jewish slave laborers (p. 51). Today, these underground tunnels have attained notoriety in Poland and have become tourist destinations. Through Riese, Kaiser learns about an "alternate Poland, where the history was of a different mode, a different mood . . . in this alternate Poland, World War II history was shiny and adventurous, all about mystery and treasure" (p. 52). One of the largest Riese sites, Wlodarz, is operated by an explorer who has turned the site into a kind of bizarre military theme park (p. 87). Now that the victims and enemy of World War II are gone, Kaiser questions as to whether a new history of World War II is being written when tourists react in awe and ambition to the Riese project (p. 63) rather than being stirred by the tragic history of the slave laborers who built Riese.

The themes of place, history, truth, and memory are further explored through Kaiser's encounters with Nazi treasure hunters/explorers. In Poland, treasure hunting for World War II artifacts is a regulated activity, meaning the government stipulates what the explorers can keep and the amount that they are compensated for World War II artifacts. This creates a culture of profiteers who are largely in the business of finding and selling artifacts from World War I and World War II. The investigation of his family's ancestry leads Kaiser to become drawn to the culture of Nazi treasure hunters/explorers because even though their "ambitions . . . were very different" (p. 52), he feels that on some level they are similar as they are both hunting and searching for answers. His Silesian guide, Joanna, introduces Kaiser to two Nazi explorers, Andrzej and Janek, who give him firsthand insight into the mindset of Nazi treasure hunters. As Kaiser rides in a car with them on a trip to Sobon, a small underground complex within Riese, Kaiser is perplexed by the "Nazi tchotchkes scattered" about in Andrzej's car, hoping that the items meant something different to Andrzej than they meant to him (p. 55). Kaiser concludes that the vast majority of Nazi explorers "are hobbyists with . . . more complex motivations—an unstable mix of pride, delusion, greed, curiosity, camaraderie, destiny, responsibility, adventure" and also a desire for fun (p. 87). Kaiser eventually joins a major exploration at a camp site during which Kaiser prods the Nazi explorers about their perception of the site and learns that for the Nazi explorers, this site is both "a site of mystery and a site of death" and that Nazi explorers can hold both truths simultaneously without many qualms (p. 162). Kaiser, however, clearly sees the painful connection between Nazi brutality and Nazi treasure but realizes for others it depends on "where the emphasis is placed" for in this alternate Poland the story of the Jews and their suffering during World War II is "abstract and incidental" (p. 52). Whereas the Nazi explorers/treasure hunters view their artifacts as an exciting type of "plunder" from a fallen enemy, Kaiser muses as to whether Nazi artifacts such as swastikas, glass eyes formerly belonging to Nazi officers, and guns can in fact be ethically viewed artifacts. For this reader, learning about the culture of Nazi exploration and Nazi treasure hunting was eye-opening.

Within the book is a section in which Kaiser has external and internal dialogues about the ethics of property reclamation, and both sides of the debate are carefully considered. Kaiser views his family's claim as "an act of justice" (p. 71) and "an inheritance claim" (p. 76). When Kaiser speaks about his reclamation attempts with friends and acquaintances, he is often met with negative reactions due to the effect his reclamation will have on the current tenants of his family's building. They argue that due to the amount of time that has passed and that so many Jews were dislocated as result of World War II, that Kaiser is not justified in seeking to reclaim his inheritance rights. Kaiser's rebuttal is that the "delay of the process" should have no bearing on the ethics of it (p. 73) and that the fact that many people suffered an injustice does not mean that justice should be denied to all (p. 74). The discussions about reclamation and its ethics are very timely, and it could serve as the basis for a high school or adult education class.

*Plunder* is in fact partially a memoir, and Kaiser's family history brings a personal, meaningful dimension to the story. Kaiser's father questions Kaiser's newfound interest in his grandfather's history and his grandfather's former attempts to reclaim the physical property and poignantly remarks to Kaiser, "Because this is not what he [Kaiser's grandfather] would have cared about . . . this is not what I wanted you to inherit" (p. 132). At one point in the book, a Nazi treasure hunter questions Kaiser's motivations at the camp exploration, and when Kaiser answers that he is there because of his grandfather's cousin, the Nazi explorer asks simply yet deeply, "You don't have family that is closer?" (p. 160), causing Kaiser to reflect and compare his link to his family's past to his relationship with his family and heritage in the present. Kaiser eventually concludes that his attempt to assert his family's rights to their property in Poland is about more than just a building, that the process is a vehicle to link himself to his ancestry and identity. At the end of the book, Kaiser muses over the different themes and possible genres of the book and philosophically concludes, "Our stories are not extensions of our grandparents' stories, are not sequels. We do not continue their stories; we act upon them" (p. 253). These few lines seem to call out to the next generation, and this reader was left pondering if the next generation will, like Kaiser, choose to "act" and assert their spiritual legacy, and if so, how they will do so. Kaiser's journey represents each generation's challenge to meaningfully attach themselves to their spiritual inheritance.

Kaiser devotes a concise section of the book to conspiracy theorists about Riese—a section that every Jewish professional should read to gain a greater understanding about Holocaust revisionism. When Kaiser first encountered these theories, his first instinct was "not necessarily to ignore but certainly not to engage" (p. 112), a common reaction to which this reader could relate. As incomprehensible as these theories may be, Kaiser found that he could not ignore them because it was "too prominent a part of Riese mythology" to disregard (p. 113). What Kaiser learns through his research is that Project Riese is the center for all sorts of outlandish beliefs about the Nazis (p. 114). Kaiser demonstrates how frightening these theories are because conspiracy theorists subscribe to a system of beliefs that create a new kind of "para history" about the Holocaust (p. 112), one that "reshapes the Holocaust . . . with little mention of any Nazi wrongdoing" (p. 119). Eventually, one finds that conspiracy theories about World War II are not just bizarre or fanciful belief systems but are "positively soaked through with anti-Semitism" (p. 120). Kaiser plainly yet seriously notes that "ideas have effects . . . and can have serious consequences," and he makes a chilling, direct link to the effects of conspiracy theories and the recent rise of horrific acts of antisemitism. This small section of *Plunder* could not be more relevant, and it should be recommended reading for anyone who cares about and identifies with Judaism.

It is often said that great learning begins with asking questions. If so, *Plunder* opens the door to great learning by its readers, for the reader will conclude the book with many questions and a desire to learn more about Holocaust history and how it is being understood by the present generation in Poland. Through the gifted writing that recounts his personal journey, Kaiser may inspire others to assert their own spiritual claim to Judaism and/or their own spiritual legacy, which in modern times would be an admirable feat. *Plunder* is a densely packed personal narrative that explores weighty themes such as the meaning of place, history, memory, truth, and family, all of which will reverberate in the reader's mind long after the narrative itself concludes.

### Note

1. Dani Shapiro, *Inheritance: A Memoir of Genealogy, Paternity, and Love* (New York: Anchor, 2020).

---

RABBI WENDY PEIN is the director of congregational learning at Temple Israel of Northern Westchester (TINW) in Croton-on-Hudson, New York, and co-president of the Westchester Association of Temple Educators. She received her MARE through the Executive Master's Program in Jewish Education from HUC-JIR.

*A Rooster for Asklepios*
by Christopher D. Stanley
(Buffalo, NY: NFB Publishing, 2020), iii + 520 pp.

*A Bull for Pluto*
by Christopher D. Stanley
(Buffalo, NY: NFB Publishing, 2020), 325 pp.

Authors across many generations have exploited the perils of travel to enliven drama and develop characters. Constant changes in setting add color to a narrative, while a plot's progress from place to place allows for mirror developments in a protagonist's own inward journey. Examples abound: Tom Joad, Huck Finn, Candide, Don Quixote, Gilgamesh, Odysseus.

To this long list of itinerant protagonists, we may now add Lucius Coelius Felix and his dutiful Jewish slave, Marcus. In *A Rooster for Asklepios* and *A Bull for Pluto*, the first two in a series of three novels comprising *A Slave's Story Trilogy* (the third installment, *A Ram for Mars*, is currently in progress), Christopher D. Stanley takes readers on a road trip through western Asia Minor in the first century CE, across its rugged mountainous routes and inside the bustling cities that dotted its landscape.

Stanley is not a novelist by trade. He has enjoyed a long and distinguished career as professor of early Christianity and the Greco-Roman world at St. Bonaventure University. It is no common feat that he has so ably adapted his historical expertise to a genre that allows him to depict the day-to-day life of urban antiquity with a measure of detail, intrigue, and appeal not attainable in an academic book or article. For readers who enjoy historical novels, and the still rarer treat of a novel set in antiquity with Jewish characters and subject matter, these new books are most welcome.

The story centers around the household of Lucius, a wealthy, widowed, Roman aristocrat residing in Antioch-near-Pisidia, a minor city in central Anatolia. Among the members of his household are Gaius, his prodigal son; Marcus, the adroit slave who operates his business; and Selena, the beautiful slave he takes for a wife. The plot turns on the stomach ailment that has already plagued Lucius for months when the story begins. After the local physicians and temple priests tell him they can offer nothing to cure him, and little more to ease his terrible suffering, Lucius resolves to pack a pair of wagons and set off for the renowned temple of Asklepios in the city of Pergamon, three hundred miles to the west. Hence the title of the first volume, *A Rooster for Asklepios*, a reference to the sacrifice offered to the god of healing. The second volume recounts the return voyage to Antioch-near-Pisidia, which includes a sojourn in the city of Hierapolis and a visit to its Ploutonion, the site of the sensational ancient festival during which priests of the goddess Cybele cheated death by surviving in a cave filled with noxious gases. The bull that entered the cave with them was not so fortunate; he was *A Bull for Pluto*, the god of the underworld.

Of interest to readers of this journal will be the depictions of Jews and Judaism that become increasingly integrated into the plot as it develops. Jews surface already in the first few pages, when leaders of the Jewish community of Antioch approach Lucius, a wealthy, civic officeholder, for support in erecting a new synagogue. Though initially reluctant, owing to his low opinion of Jews informed by popular stereotypes of the day, Lucius figures that partnership with the local Jews might be a worthwhile political risk. What ensues is a relationship with a network of Jewish associates that sees him staying in three Jewish homes along his journey, first in the great city of Ephesus, then in Pergamon, and then once more in Hierapolis. Over time, Lucius realizes that Jews are not nearly the reprehensible lot he had been led to imagine.

Far more profound is the transformation in his slave, Marcus, who comes to learn that he is in fact of Jewish ancestry. (Slaves often knew nothing of their parents, especially their fathers.) The revelation about his parentage comes at the end of the first volume, though it is hinted at from the very first page. The second volume sees Marcus struggling extensively with his newfound Jewish identity and its implications for his continued worship of the gods, his loyalty to his master, and ultimately the romantic relationship he forges with Miriam, a Jewish slave from Hierapolis. Without revealing too much about what transpires, my understanding is that the third volume will see Marcus and Miriam in Judea on the eve of the revolt against Rome.

Stanley is an illustrious scholar, as I mentioned, and as a result these novels inform and educate as much as they entertain. Turning each page is like walking from exhibit to exhibit at a living history museum. So much of what we know about Hellenized Asia Minor is brought to life: the role of class in Greco-Roman society, and in particular the institution of slavery; the ins and outs of pagan religion, both at temples and in the household; the precariousness of travel between cities; the ancient healing arts; baths, theaters, urban festivals; and important legal matters such as adoption, inheritance, manumission, and marriage. Stanley depicts each of these with the deftness of a scholar well acquainted with the wide array of literary and archaeological sources available. It is true that on occasion the reader might sense the professor pushing the novelist aside—a few pages are more lecture than literature—but these moments are few and far between. Reading these novels is indeed like reading novels, not like taking a course. The novels are nonetheless mixed through and through with history. Readers will witness the past brought to life vividly and accurately, which is precisely what fans of historical novels want to see.

For Jewish book clubs, adult education groups, students in literature or history courses, or just your run-of-the-mill history buffs, *A Slave's Story Trilogy* is worth a look.

RABBI JOSHUA GARROWAY, PhD, serves as the Sol and Arlene Bronstein Professor of Judaeo-Christian Studies and professor of Early Christianity and Second Commonwealth Judaism at HUC-JIR/Los Angeles. Rabbi Garroway was ordained at HUC-JIR/Cincinnati in 2003 and earned his doctorate from Yale University in 2008. His books and scholarly articles focus on the emergence of Christianity against the backdrop of Second Temple and Rabbinic Judaism.

*The Jews Should Keep Quiet: Franklin D. Roosevelt, Rabbi Stephen S. Wise, and the Holocaust*
by Rafael Medoff
(Philadelphia: The Jewish Publication Society, 2019), 387 pp.

We are greatly indebted to Professor Rafael Medoff, an Orthodox ordained rabbi and prolific author, who serves as the founding director of the David S. Wyman Institute for Holocaust Studies as well as the co-editor of its online Encyclopedia of American Response to the Holocaust. How instructive and natural that *The Jews Should Keep Quiet* is dedicated to the late Wyman, whose breakthrough 1984 book, *The Abandonment of the Jews*, charted a pioneering and courageous path of consequential and painful realities in confronting the Shoah's monumental dimensions.

The availability of revealing new material unfortunately helps demonstrate beyond doubt, in Medoff's masterfully-researched and painstakingly-weaved study, that Franklin D. Roosevelt and Rabbi Stephen S. Wise's policies of commission and omission contributed to an overwhelming calamity for the Jewish people and humanity. Medoff succeeds in debunking long-held views such as that FDR, who was practically worshiped by adoring American Jews for his New Deal, cared for Jews and their preeminent leader, Rabbi Wise. Emerging is a Machiavellian plot to cynically outmaneuver a naively trusting Jewish leader who was enamored by a clever president who bestowed upon Wise and his family tokens of friendship and gratitude, ensnaring Wise to believe that FDR would not betray him and even more critically, a vulnerable European Jewry in Hitler's devouring clutches.

In fact, unwittingly or not, Wise enabled FDR, "a master manipulator" (p. xii), in his constant intimidating harangue "that he wanted the Jews to keep quiet" (p. 309) and their obeyed silence would best serve to save fellow Jews and even protect American Jews in a highly antisemitic society, which by 1940 had more than one hundred antisemitic organizations with the vast popularity of the antisemitic Catholic priest Father Charles Coughlin. Isolationism, nativism, and, following the Great Depression, high unemployment were important factors to contend with, and as Medoff points out in FDR's defense, weighed on him while also burdened with World War II preparations. Thus, Wise did all in his substantial power to enforce Jewish fatal inaction as leader of the major Jewish organizations: the American Jewish Congress, which he founded to neutralize the then anti-Zionist American Jewish Committee; the World Jewish Congress; the Jewish Institute of Religion, which he founded and later merged with the Hebrew Union College; and he was also chief editor of the magazine *Opinion*.

To aggravate matters, FDR's mom, Sarah, and other family members were unabashedly antisemitic. FDR himself was proud of his family being devoid of "Jewish blood," and he was reluctant to bestow on his fifth child the Hebrew name Isaac. He explained away Polish antisemitism to the dismayed though loyal Wise, saying that it resulted from Jewish prominence, "the Jewish grain dealer and the Jewish shoe dealer and the Jewish shopkeeper" (p. 73). Looking down on Jews (envy, perhaps?) went along with ill-feelings toward Asians with the likely connection to the internment of over 120,000 American Japanese during the war. How else explain the 1939 sordid affair of FDR turning away the SS *St. Louis* though the US Virgin Islands offered safe haven to the 937 desperate fleeing Jewish refugees? How else understand that FDR opposed, aiding and abetting a notorious antisemitic State Department, in eleven of his twelve years in office (1933–1945), to fulfill the quota for Germany, and his refusal to accept 20,000 Jewish German children? Vice President Henry Wallace quotes Secretary of War Henry Stimson that the State Department is "the wailing wall for Jews" (p. 240).

Three days before Yom Kippur on October 6, 1943, the first Jewish march on Washington took place with over four hundred Orthodox rabbis participating to Wise's chagrin. Organized by the Bergson Group, this massive demonstration of very traditional rabbis in practice and appearance, who spoke Yiddish and represented a distinct old world Jewish flavor that made Wise and fully acculturated American Jews very uncomfortable and ever concerned of how the non-Jews would react. The goal of this impressive turnout of spiritual leaders on behalf of their millions of European brethren sought to pressure FDR's Administration to create an agency focused on rescuing the threatened Jews from extinction. Fearing embarrassment and worse, FDR chose the meek approach of avoidance and refused to even meet with the rabbis' delegation and hear it out.

It was only under the cloud of a likely adoption of a congressional resolution to firmly support Jewish refugees and with a pending election did the ever-self-serving FDR agree to reverse course and establish the War Refugee Board (WRB) with Executive Order 9417 on January 23, 1944. Treasury Secretary Henry Morgenthau Jr., the only Jew to ever serve in an FDR cabinet, was instrumental, to his credit, in FDR's long-coming acquiescence in saving Jewish lives but at what delayed cost! It is telling that at a prior critical meeting with FDR, Morgenthau told the president that his father, Morgenthau Sr., helped those victimized in the Ottoman's Armenian genocide. Yet, the tragic delay amounted to a loss of more than four million Jewish lives and 440,000 Hungarian Jews. The celebrated Raul Wallenberg was recruited and supported by WRB's agent in Sweden, Iver Olsen. Medoff rightly emphasizes that since the WRB managed to save 200,000 Jews and 20,000 non-Jews till the war's end in May 1945—numbers that pale in comparison to the vast losses—it is proof that had the WRB been established earlier it would have made a significant difference. FDR's claim that because his administration's mantra with Wise buying into it, that Jewish rescue should await Nazism's defeat, proved to be false and disastrous.

Liberty ships transporting American troops to Europe and returning home empty could have carried refugees had there been a will. The failure of responding to Jewish pleas to bomb the railways and bridges leading to Auschwitz and the murder of 1.1 million Jews, in the guise that aerial military operations took precedence, has no justification. Allied planes dropped bombs on enemy oil and chemical installations nearby. On August 20, 1944, a major American bombing campaign raided targets five miles from Auschwitz with the participation of the famed African American

Tuskegee Airmen piloting 100 Mustang fighters. Sixteen-year-old prisoner Elie Wiesel witnessed it with joy and later bemoaning in his classic *Night* that no bombs rained on Auschwitz.

Medoff refers to Wise's neglect early on to form coalitions with both Christians and Jews, ever concerned with retaining his sole leadership power and guarding his patron FDR's passive-evasive approach. Wise was consumed with fighting the activist Bergson Group that generated some two hundred full-page ads in major newspapers such as the *New York Times*, with the driving goal of saving lives and the creation of a Jewish state in Palestine. It was led by Hillel Kook, the firebrand nephew of then-Palestine's chief rabbi, whom he protected with the pseudonym "Bergson." The group, the brainchild of the Revisionist leader Zeev Jabotinsky, attracted the likes of the screen writer Ben Hecht and was thoroughly investigated by the FBI and the IRS with no incriminating outcome. Another target of Wise's watchful eye was the emerging brilliant orator Rabbi Abba Hillel Silver, whom he regarded as his "archenemy" (p. 254) and primary Zionist leadership competitor. Silver did not mince words either. The author regrets that Wise did not take advantage of opportunities to intervene on behalf of European Jewry with the 1943 shifting tide of war, which wise leaders would have utilized. Wise is blamed for his inability to free himself from his all-consuming allegiance to FDR. Perhaps, muses Medoff, Wise's increasing health issues were a factor. A persisting puzzle: To what extent was FDR and for that matter Rabbi Wise victimized products of their times, and to what degree did they fail to rise above their times and truly make a critical difference?

Following the February 1945 Yalta Conference, FDR met with Saudi Arabia's King Ibn Saud aboard the USS *Quincey*, at which both of them nixed the revival of Jewish life in Palestine. It is safe to conjecture that had FDR been in office in 1948, he would not vote for the declared Jewish State. Already in spring 1938 the both visionary and practical David Ben- Gurion called FDR "an anti-Zionist" (p. 226). Rabbi Dr. Israel Goldstein, who led the Synagogue Council of America along with the Zionist Organization of America, though he worked with Wise and admired him, sensed that vulnerable Wise fell for FDR's superb spell. Goldstein later reflected, "Thus in the end, six million Jews perished while the United States dithered and temporized, while the British doggedly sealed off ports of embarkation, and while we Jews in the Free

World naively heeded assurances that 'everything possible would be done' to save lives" (p. 305).

In his 1949 autobiography, *Challenging Years*, Wise seals his positive evaluation of FDR with glowing words though Medoff interprets it as opening a window for potential criticism of his idolized hero. Thus, Wise seeks to defend his own blemished record that cannot be separated from FDR's indefensible record. "'It is in his rendezvous with destiny that he was equal to its measureless and majestic responsibility. Woe to them who vainly sought and seek to divert this heroic figure from his definitely appointed rendezvous'" (p. 306).

The author should be commended for an essential study shedding further light on a watershed period, attempting a challenging balanced approach with irrefutable evidence condemning two major figures whose close collaboration ultimately carried disastrous consequences. Medoff deliberately concludes, "He [FDR] saw America as 'a Protestant country' with 'the Jews' and people of other backgrounds present only 'on sufferance.' Perhaps, then, it is not surprising that he was disposed to policies that would exclude, restrict, dispense, or silence such minorities. To stifle Jewish criticism of these policies, Roosevelt exploited the insecurities of a mostly immigrant and not yet fully accepted community and maneuvered Rabbi Wise to help ensure that the Jews would keep quiet" (pp. 314–15).

---

RABBI DR. ISRAEL ZOBERMAN (C74) is founder and spiritual leader of Temple Lev Tikvah in Virginia Beach, Virginia. He is Honorary Senior Rabbi Scholar at Eastern Shore Chapel Episcopal Church in Virginia Beach. He and his family of Polish Holocaust survivors lived from 1945 to 1949 among refugees in Kazakhstan (USSR), Poland, Austria, and Germany.


*Bait Shlishi—Meam Lishvatin Leam* (The Third Commonwealth— From a Nation to Tribes to a Nation)
by Ari Shavit*
(Rishon LeZion, Israel: Miskal-Yedioth Ahronoth Books and Chemed Books, 2021), 221 pp. (in Hebrew)

The English title given to this original and essential book, *A New Israeli Republic*, is an inspiring contribution within the praiseworthy Beit Yotzer Yisraeli (Israeli Creator's Association) of distinguished thinkers along with movers and shakers on the Israeli scene who are deeply concerned about as well as sincerely committed to the state of the State of Israel's well-being. Their guiding thesis is the Jewish state's internal disintegration as its major challenge, that if continued unchecked might lead to catastrophic consequences and even to the destruction of the Third Jewish Commonwealth and the cessation of a Jewish future. What an ominous and far-reaching conclusion, perhaps designed to shock us into action. The thorough analysis of Israel's fragmentary ailments offers a way out based on the founding of a centrally broad Zionist stream that will serve to unify the disparate tribalism threatening the state's very survival that early on David Ben-Gurion feared and thus insisting on a framework of *mamlachtiyut*, proper statehood structure and conduct based on majority rule and state interests.

Veteran Israeli author and journalist Ari Shavit, a graduate of The Hebrew University of Jerusalem, whose 2013 best seller *My Promised Land* was translated into many languages and won him the National Jewish Book Award for history, shares with both over-following pride and painful apprehension:

> For me, the State of Israel is a miracle performed by human be-ings. No other country did what we have done. No democratic country has prospered like ours in such a hostile environment. Despite all the enemies, wars, troubles, failures and mistakes— the Zionist dream is fulfilled. Our sons and daughters have in the forefathers' land what our grandfathers and grandmothers lacked: Sovereignty, liberty, honor, pride and progress. However, in recent years we all sense that something has gone awry. Though Israel is a rare success story—Israel is also torn, wounded, hurt-ing and bleeding. It lost its way. (p. 12)

While the roots of modern Israel are in a secular worldview that consciously removed itself from the traditional underpinnings of past Jewish believing, living, and survival, we witness a growing and promising synthesis, points out the author, between the em-brace of the benefits of the contemporary technological revolution and becoming a start-up nation with a yearning to creatively re-connect to the past treasures of Jewish learning and the support-ive warmth of its communal expression, the *k'hilah* in a modern context of voluntary affiliation in pluralistic settings. An important by-product of this trend is easing the alienating tension between secular Zionism and Religious Orthodox Zionism:

It is somewhat like a culture of children who turned their back to all their parents' worlds, spontaneously founding a new improvised world of their own. A world that doesn't obey the *Shulchan Aruch*, and doesn't fulfill Herzl's vision, and doesn't realize Ben-Gurion's master plan. But a world that the *Shulchan Aruch*, Herzl and Ben-Gurion are folded within it. A world that fully lives the inner contradictions of the Zionist enterprise and the Israeli reality. Trying to turn forced limitations into springboards, weaknesses into strengths and disasters into opportunities, using materials found on the beach to which it was swept to create an improvised something complicated, confusing and colorful that is full of magic that is the Israel of the third millennium. (p. 129)

The early British influence on the Zionist Movement gave way with Israel's establishment to the French one and then to a dominating American culture, which Shavit, while acknowledging its pervasive impact also offers critical reservations on its full suitability to a beleaguered small country in the Middle East. From a necessary strategic alliance with the United States, the author questions the degree to which Israel is imitating all things American. In the process, I believe that his blanket condemnation does not do justice to the American system with its magnificent accomplishments, rather focusing on shortcomings glaringly made manifest recently and the failure to fully live up to the glorious promise of the American dream. After all, the still young and noble American experiment is a work in progress. Shavit does not mince words, arousing the suspicion that his overreaction of an analytical mind hides some personal misgivings:

The American worship has become the new Israeli religion. Without a conscious decision, Israel actually replaced its disintegrating old model with the American one. It has attempted to build a state based on the individual (now turned king), on the financial markets (now turned into a sacred church) and on the constitution (advanced by Israel's basic laws and supreme court chief justice Barak's revolution). A new world of American ideas replaced the old Israeli one. An American value system replaced the Zionist-Israeli one. The Americanization radically changed Israel's character. But the American model doesn't fit the Israeli situation. It lacks mutual responsibility along with social justice, communal cohesiveness, human warmth, sense of family and trust. (p.135)

What a list of misleading and exaggerated woes leading to wrong evaluations!

Shavit rightly and enthusiastically lauds Israel's pioneering success in its admirable response to the COVID-19 crisis that illustrates the country at its best. He recommends and urges that this kind of exemplar service to the individual and society should become a model for all other societal aspects that the Israel government provides and is responsible for. Yet, he does not hesitate to designate the current Israeli capitalistic state as a "Sinful state— *Medinat Avlah*" (p. 162), given the growing dangerous gap between a very wealthy minority of mostly high-tech beneficiaries and the struggling rest of the country facing a tough economy that fails to match the high cost of Israeli living, exacerbated during the COVID-19 pandemic with the disastrous layoffs of significant numbers. These economical and societal extremes contribute to a fragmentation that Israel cannot afford, given its existential dilemmas.

Looking forward to Israel's hundredth anniversary in 2048, the author calls for replacing Ben-Gurion's foundational framework of centralized rule favoring the East European Ashkenazim and demoting the Arab countries' Mizrachim with a kind of hyphenated citizenship acknowledging and celebrating all those living in the Jewish and democratic Israel—that should thus retain its Jewish majority—with the variety of traditions represented, allowing for an inclusive and heterogeneous Israeli culture to flourish, the one that Ben-Gurion resented in the early stage of nation-building.

The new complex hyphenated Israeli identity will include one and all: A Chareidi Israeli, an Arab Israeli, a Mizrachi Israeli, a gay Israeli, a liberal Israeli, a conservative Israeli, and so forth with full equality for women. Israel will also assist in gradually, stage by stage, providing for a Palestinian state, one that will not undermine Israeli's security.

The author calls for establishing a joint Israeli-Diaspora peace corps in which the Jewish youth from the two interdependent Jewish centers will collaboratively engage in projects promoting and enhancing Jewish and universal values in Israel, the United States, and around the world. A great, ambitious idea indeed! This constructive and demanding approach, "thus, in the eyes of liberal Jewish youth in the Diaspora, Israel will no longer be identified with occupation, oppression, fanaticism and reactionism, rather with human rights, social justice and environmentalism, allowing the Z-generation to combine its universal values with an open Judaism and enlightened Israel. The Jewish peace corps will become a somewhat new Taglit project that will try to turn the world into a better place while connecting the Israeli youth with its Diaspora counterpart on the basis of meaningful voluntary work along with serious Jewish study and Ahavat Yisrael—naturally loving fellow Jews" (p. 209). Overall, Shavit perceives Israel as a better-equipped partner in this grand enterprise since the Diaspora, particularly its non-Orthodox and liberal segments, is in the throes of assimilation and rapid decline. Granted, there is bias in this oversimplified perspective.

The author's fruitful vision, with a prophetic dimension, is a tall order but a necessary one. Even if only some of it will be fulfilled, it would be a significant accomplishment—worthy projects that bring closer Jewish youth at risk of growing apart, thus granting an indispensable service in furthering Jewish unity and guaranteeing the Jewish future. At stake, quite convincingly claims the author, no less than Israel's very survival for a Fourth Jewish Commonwealth is not an option. Indeed, this arousing book is a lovers' quarrel for Israel and the Jewish people's sake. In a way Israel is a victim of its own success. Shavit's semi-utopian plan for Israel includes a new leadership that is removed from sectarian politics following the biblical Levites model, whose transcendent concern for their people is sought by Shavit to create an Israeli society that is a guiding shining lighthouse also for humanity at large. He concludes on a realistic, yet sobering note, "I am optimistic I believe in the Israeli person and the Israeli spirit. In our beloved land there are countless human treasures and forces of light that can be actualized. But the time has come to tackle it seriously, earnestly, for there won't be a fourth commonwealth. Israel is the last opportunity —and a wonderful one—of the Jewish people" (p. 220). Amen.

*Ari Shavit resigned in 2016 from both *Haaretz* newspaper and Israeli TV Channel 10 following accusations of sexual assault by two American Jewish women.

---

RABBI DR. ISRAEL ZOBERMAN (C74) is founder and spiritual leader of Temple Lev Tikvah in Virginia Beach, Virginia. He is honorary senior rabbi scholar at Eastern Shore Chapel Episcopal Church in Virginia Beach. He is a past member of the *CCAR Journal*'s editorial board and translated all the quotes.

*Shake and Tremor*
by Deborah Bacharach
(West Hartford, CT: Grayson Books, 2021), 78 pp.

Deborah Bacharach's latest book of poetry highlights women's inner lives and thoughts. She writes about biblical women whose names we know, like Sarah and Hagar, as well as those whose names we do not know and whose voices we do not hear: Potiphar's wife, Lot's wife, Lot's daughters. While classical midrash often uses the first-person voice to give us men's thoughts and perspectives in the context and idioms of the writers' times and cultures, even many modern midrashim that seek to include women do not assume the woman's voice. Rather, they read between the lines of the text to tell us about these women; Bacharach does this, too, but she also wants us to hear them for ourselves.

Here is Hagar, as Bacharach hears her:

Tonight I walk into the desert
with one sack of water and my son.
My body an ocean I move
with the moon. I did not demand a promise.
I did not ask for my son, Ishmael

already curled in a grave-like hollow.
An angel visits me on this road to Beersheba.
Angel is the word I say when I mean
strength of will, deep and abiding conviction.
Angel is the word I say when I hear
water rise up in the well.

Hagar is a survivor. She may be a pawn in a larger story, one that is not her story, as we have it in the Torah, but she is not passive. She does not give up her sense of self and her right to understand her life on her own terms.

Nor do the other biblical women to whom Bacharach gives shape and voice. Did Lot's wife look back?

". . . I tripped. I caught a flash and thought

my wedding ring. I could picture
my knitting,
My frail peonies . . .

Lot's wife, his daughters, and Lot himself all come under Bacharach's unflinching eye. They are weak, they are practical, they may or may not be like the rest of their neighbors in Sodom and Gomorrah, and yet they are very much a part of the destruction. Are we moved by their weakness and casual cruelty, or by their enduring humanity?

And what was Mrs. Potiphar thinking when she tried to seduce Joseph? She watches him tend to her husband's needs, and finds him irresistible, even as he resists her. She knows he is forbidden, and yet:

> I saw the oasis
> shimmer at the edge of the horizon
> like I had been walking toward it
> my entire life, like I had been crawling
> on my hands and knees.

There are midrashim in various collections that give us a story about Mrs. Potiphar inviting a group of women to her home and serving them something to eat, with knives for cutting their food. She brings Joseph in front of them so that they can see his beauty for themselves; they are so taken with him that they cannot focus on the fruit, but cut their hands instead.[1] In Bacharach's poem, Mrs. Potiphar describes her desire, and we understand.

Bacharach uses modern idioms to retell biblical stories and to create windows into the lives of the people we encounter in our sacred text. As our commentators have always done, she wants to see them as three-dimensional characters, whose feelings and needs we can understand, because they are like us. We learn the lessons of human relationships from them precisely because they are so human.

But bringing our ancestors into the twenty-first century does not absolve them of their flaws. They are perhaps more recognizable in translation, but we also see how alike we are, particularly in the harsh light of our own cynical, expedient, and self-dealing choices. Here are excerpts from "How Do You Justify Yourself?"

> Bash the attacker—that's justifiable
> self-defense perhaps. But if you shoot
> his brothers, cousins, divorced first wife,
> random small children just in case, then
> defense is just the excuse you give
> to lick fresh blood from your fingertips . . .

Ah yes, those fill-in-the-blanks (spit when you say it)
They are not your neighbors—the woman who bought milk,
The boy who drew spirals. They are monsters,
ogres. They have come from the bowels
of the earth. You, with a baby strapped to your back,
grab that axe, attack . . .

None of which explains, Lot
offering his daughters to the mob.

Bacharach challenges us: can we turn the mirror around to look at ourselves?

There are also poems about modern relationships that are not drawn from the Torah. There is love, marriage, motherhood, and loss. There is passion and regret. At times, Bacharach writes with almost a Sondheim-esque sense of fallibility and with bittersweet recognition that not everybody lives happily ever after, but most people go on living. They may even look back on past happiness without regret—and keep striving.

All of this is more than we
can understand, we who are hungry,
come further than we can
fathom. I declare all can,
should, will.

### Note

1. James L. Kugel, *In Potiphar's House* (Cambridge: Harvard University Press, 1994), 28–33.

RABBI BETH SCHWARTZ is rabbi emerita of Temple Israel of Columbus, Georgia. She has contributed to *The Women's Haftarah Commentary* and the forthcoming *Prophetic Voices: Renewing and Reimagining Haftarah*.

*Nahum, Habakkuk, and Zephaniah: Lights in the Valley*
by Yaakov Beasley
(New Milford, CT, and Jerusalem: Maggid Books, 2020), 262 pp.

The biblical books Nahum, Habakkuk, and Zephaniah are not the most popular. For good reason: They are short, which gives a feeling that they are incomplete.

Their subject matter is so off putting. Nahum speaks in terms of harsh vengeance without the opportunity for redemption. Habakkuk complains. Zephaniah's "day of the Lord" is so grim, viewed by many scholars as one of the darkest verses of the Bible. Still, this is part of the tradition we received.

Yaakov Beasley wrote *Nahum, Habakkuk, and Zephaniah: Lights in the Valley* as a quest to find the meaning in that which is easy to overlook. This is not for the beginner. There are many other parts of *Tanach* that are so much more accessible, whose message easily resonates with us today. This is for the connoisseur. If you are looking to mine gold from remote and difficult shafts, this is your book.

Rabbi Beasley has Reform roots and Orthodox academic training. He really wants us to understand the politics of the day so we can see the biblical words in their contemporary context. This book is as much a history of Assyria and Babylonia as it is about the prophets.

Each prophet is given a separate section of the book. Chapters deal with history, complete running commentary, and a conclusion filled with takeaways. These books show us that there is no uniform job description for a biblical prophet.

Did you know that Nahum was referred to as a poet-laureate because of his mastery of language: using gender to give voice, alliteration, acrostic, assonance, consonance, and word play? This gives the feeling that the words should be vocalized, not simply read. Habakkuk encourages us to use our anger to question norms of the day. He has a transformation resulting in beautiful praises of God's work. Zephaniah uses strong language to motivate us to repent, showing the power of hope.

As Reform rabbis, we need to deal with all the facets of Judaism we inherited. We are powerful when we bring the prominent sacred texts to our people in a way that they can grow from. We are authentic when we are aware of the least prominent texts and have a way to deal with them. This book familiarizes us with three of the least prominent books of our bible. If we call them our sacred text, then we need to be familiar with them and use them to further our spiritual goals.

It is easy to cite these texts as ones we reject. It is even easier to pass them over, without comment. It is hard to work them into our belief that every generation of our people felt that these were sacred treasures worth passing on to the next generation. That's where this book is most helpful.

If our classes and sermons were like plates of food we prepare and serve for others' nourishment, *Nahum, Habakkuk, and Zephaniah: Lights in the Valley* provides rare ingredients that make the whole dish stand out.

RABBI JEFFREY GLICKMAN (C87) received his MBA from UConn in 2009 and DD from HUC-JIR in 2012, and he serves Temple Beth Hillel in South Windsor, Connecticut. Jeff is the author of *Have You Heard?*, an adult book disguised as a children's book about the Ten Commandments, and several licensed board games. He and his wife, Mindy, continue to be amazed by their seven children and their spouses.

# Poetry

# Have a Nice Trip,
# See You Next Fall

*Matthue Roth*

*You're doing so*
*well* you tell
me, and add the
unspoken suffix:
*considering*

You're so happy I'm
spreading lights
moving mountains
but I wish I could
tell you it's
a lie

I've been bleeding so bad
all I can do is
suck it like a vampire

Both polymath and underachiever,
in every field I score, and score poorly
not always there when you call

My prayer to G-d
for deliverance from danger is really
*How the hell have I made it this far*

The answer comes
as clear as heaven looks from afar
the day after you die:
*you did*

MATTHUE ROTH is the author of the poetry collection *Somehow I Have Built a Nest* (bit.ly/some-how) and the novel *Never Mind the Goldbergs*. He created the web series Bimbam and wrote the voice of the Google Assistant. He keeps a secret diary at matthue.com, and lives with his daughters in Brooklyn.

# Samson's Mother

*Patty Seyburn, PhD*

All superheroes need
a great origin story,
even one poorly edited.

In the movie, he was played
by Victor Mature. In the Rubens
painting, he wrestles a lion.

This representation is accurate.
This depiction is accurate.
Don't we all want our children

to do better? To have an easier
life? Manoah said, get the angel
back down here—how do

we raise this hairy son?
The angel did not want
to speak with him, but I give

him credit for admitting
he did not know how to handle
a man destined to be

Great. The angel said its name
was unknowable. My name
is unknown, but I am no

PATTY SEYBURN, PhD, has published five collections of poems, most recently *Threshold Delivery* (Finishing Line Press, 2019). She has a PhD from University of Houston, an MFA from UC-Irvine, and an MS and BS from Northwestern University. She is a proud professor at California State University, Long Beach.

angel. I am a mother. There is
a pathway to holiness.
My son was shown it.

His name comes from the sun.
His nemesis from the night.
There are different sorts of strength.

Children get their hair
from their mothers. When you cut
hair, you are cutting something

that belongs to God. Do I
belong to God? I would like
to meet that angel again.

# Today's Flutter of Questions

I know that the sparrows are
not talking to me. Their speech
seems to favor a few key
phrases: found food, found shelter,
predator alert. Torture
that worm. Good work on that nest.
Are there arguments? Gossip?
Kvetching? Prayer? Praise? Discourse on
existence? Vacation plans?
Are some birds more voluble
than others? Snow White spoke-sang
to bluebirds. St. Francis preached
to a literal flock, "clothed
in feathers." Aidel, daughter
of the Baal Shem Tov also
conversed with avian friends.
Silence. Birds, where did you go?
I liked eavesdropping on you.

# I would like a new tree

to house my oracle
where justice can be dispensed.
On one branch grows the anodyne
On another, a plum.

My tree is my relation

My tree may be the *kikayon* that grows
over Jonah, the tree felled
by a worm

My tree may be
real, may be
symbolic, may be
imaginary

may be
a date palm, a tamarisk, even
a messy eucalyptus
perhaps an oak or sycamore or fig.

In one of the three hundred and ten
worlds beneath my tree

lives my personal Eden

I would cultivate it
I would celebrate it

There is a word for a tree
that sounds like strong
that sounds like a bone
that sounds like advice

I would not be afraid.

# Living with It

*Judith Skillman*

I listen for the kraken all night
sliding off the roof,
its legs wound around windows
and in its head the large eyes
of my past shining
bright as mercury—and has it come
to tell about fear
or the apprenticeship of sailors?
Large as an island, that sloping back
I rode as a child.
The heads and tails of a stinging thing
that once caught my legs
in the Atlantic. Mother's colander
couldn't drain the seepage
from those wounds. Even Father,
rumored to exist in his study,
had no luck with currents
of sound emanating from the melt
perhaps snow or maybe
patches of green grown through
one of its many bellies
full of man of wars.

# The Silver Lining

You find it resides with much fervor
in an old winter coat,
one of many stored
inside garment bags,
mothball moons gathered the bottom.

---

JUDITH SKILLMAN is the recipient of awards from the Academy of American Poets and Artist Trust. Her new collection is *A Landscaped Garden for the Addict* (Shanti Arts Press, 2021). Visit www.judithskillman.com.

One grandmother
stood toothless as she spat
on your head
and welcomed you into a kitchen
full of unleavened crumbs
and poppy seeds.
The other Bubba
sat with blued hair
and an inhaler, asked you
if you wanted a cough drop,
a peppermint, or a story
of Liverpool during the bombing.

You find buttercream icing
in a suitcase purse,
mohair sweaters that don't itch.
The uncles—even Julio
with his Latin rages—
gone to hell. The aunts
schmoozing color TV,
waltzing nude beneath housedresses
and smoking jackets.

# Still

*Paul Hostovsky*

When there's nothing to say there is still
this to say, still there is this like a
birdbath in someone's yard in your
childhood, not your birdbath or your yard
and no birds now, or rainwater yet, just this
palm, this listening for the rain, this memory
of a waiting place made of stone for the birds,
if they come, to drink from the rain after
a rain. When there's nothing to say there is still
this asking, this open upturned face, this mouth
waiting to collect the first few drops,
this hopeful, trembling tongue.

# The Story of the World

Praise the im-
provised, the im-
perfect, the jerry-
rigged, the jerry-
built, praise Jerry, who-
ever he was, a lands-
man after my own inept
broken heart,
which I keep trying to fix
with a little duct tape
and Elmer's glue.
Praise Elmer, praise
the tacky, tottering half-
assed job, the un-

---

PAUL HOSTOVSKY's latest book is *Deaf & Blind* (Main Street Rag, 2020). His poems have won a Pushcart Prize, two Best of the Net Awards, and have been featured on *Poetry Daily*, *Verse Daily*, and *The Writer's Almanac*. He makes his living in Boston as a sign language interpreter. His website is paulhostovsky.com.

professional, the un-
reliable, the unstable
and unsound. Praise
all the safety pins
and paper clips
and staples holding the story
of the world together,
a story that doesn't hold up
with its impossible plot
and vast cast of rickety,
flawed characters,
every last one of them un-
believable.

# Adam
# . . . and Eve

*Diana Rosen*

Some say *HaShem* fashioned Adam,
and Eve,
from clay: dust, water, His hot breath—

like an artisan designs a vase, a bowl,
things that survive The Great Fire.

Others say Adam,
and Eve,
all those who came afterward, were molded

not in His image to withstand the flames,
but to be vulnerable flesh to live life in joy.

Still others believe Adam,
and Eve,
all blood, heartbeats, breath, were created

not to offer awe to The One Unseen, but to pay
attention, love the world, each other, enough.

DIANA ROSEN is an essayist, poet, and flash fiction writer with credits in *Tiferet Journal*, *The Jewish Writing Project*, *Mizmor Anthology eCollection*, *Jewish Literary Journal*, and previous issues of *The Reform Jewish Quarterly*. To read more of her work, please visit www.authory.com/dianarosen.

# Tirza Reveals the Miraculous

*Julie R. Enszer, PhD*

Miracles in our day are minor
we lack the drama of splitting seas and burning bushes
G!d no longer appears to us dramatically

She no longer speaks directly
Sure, people sometimes see her in dreams
or glimmers of her hand in the world

but our miracles are minor
the misplaced socks that delay a day
resulting in not being on the train that crashes

the occasion of meeting a new person
who happens to introduce you to their best friend whose cousin
is your *bashert*

Miracles today are
less divinely ordained
than accidental even incidental

Even the *lamed-vavniks* who are
directly responsible for these miracles
do not recognize their own power

JULIE R. ENSZER, PhD, is the author of four poetry collections, *Avowed* (Sibling Rivalry Press, 2016), *Lilith's Demons* (A Midsummer Night's Press, 2015), *Sisterhood* (Sibling Rivalry Press, 2013), and *Handmade Love* (A Midsummer Night's Press, 2010). She is editor of *The Complete Works of Pat Parker* (Sinister Wisdom/A Midsummer Night's Press, 2016), which won the 2017 Lambda Literary Award for Lesbian Poetry and *Milk & Honey: A Celebration of Jewish Lesbian Poetry* (A Midsummer Night's Press, 2011), which was a finalist for the 2012 Lambda Literary Award in Lesbian Poetry. She has her MFA and PhD from the University of Maryland. Enszer edits and publishes *Sinister Wisdom*, a multicultural lesbian literary and art journal, and is a regular book reviewer for the *The Rumpus* and *Calyx*. You can read more of her work at www.JulieREnszer.com.

The UPS carrier who helps install the AC unit
was no simple man dressed in brown
and the miracle of the electricity was no simple electronic error

Yet why should everyone witness these miracles
Part of the miracle of the *lamed-vavniks*
is to cover up the miracles in the world

to be the just in time person
to be the physical explanation of goodness
and to refuse it

the real *lamed-vavniks*
never think they are
they always find themselves wanting

find themselves short
they would never presume
righteousness for themselves

it is the brilliant deferral by G!d
and with so many
it is always difficult to keep up

# First Light

*Elaine Terranova*

and the birds are scrambling
over who gets first say

while people who sleep rough
on the ground, do they stir
at the encouragement of morning?

I think of my brothers
praying on rising each day
of their lives thus far,

did they extract phylacteries
from the velvet pouch in a drawer

did they remember
in the forgetting wards
of nursing homes to give thanks

for the next day and the next,
strapping themselves to God
in hard leather bands?

# The Road to Gravure

At Easter, my mother washed the dishes, humming "Easter
Parade."
    "Irving Berlin was Jewish," she confided, "but he wrote
'White Christmas' and 'The Easter Parade,' the most popular

ELAINE TERRANOVA is the author of *The Diamond Cutter's Daughter: A Poet's Memoir* (Ragged Sky Press, 2021), and seven collections of poetry. Her awards include a Pushcart Prize, a Pew Fellowship, the Judah Magnus Award for a Poem on the Jewish Experience, and a National Endowment in the Arts Fellowship. Her work has appeared in *The New Yorker*, *The Cincinnati Review*, *The Alaska Quarterly Review*, and other magazines and anthologies.

songs for the gentile holidays." And to her, they weren't gentile, only popular, American.

Yet she would never sign a note allowing me to sing carols in school at Christmastime with gentile children and Jews whose parents didn't mind. A messenger, some angelic girl from the upper grades, would knock on classroom doors to gather the carolers and the rest of us listened forlornly from our desks to the silvery music streaming through the halls while we did arithmetic.

I liked to hear my mother humming over housework; it meant she was happy or at least in an easygoing mood. I especially liked how Judy Garland's voice swelled with the words when she sang "Easter Parade" in the movie. Some of the lyrics puzzled me though. "In your Easter bonnet, with all the frills upon it." A bonnet, wasn't it only for babies? And what was that "Road to Gravure"? I asked my mother and she didn't know. She thought it was maybe a place in France. Later I learned the word rotogravure, "You'll find that you're in the rotogravure," a photographic process newspapers used.

But the idea of a road to gravure stayed with me. It was a clue to the future, to how seriously life should be taken.

# It Rained All Sukkot

*Roger Nash*

nonstop cold drizzle
even flocks of mallard ducks
just can't shake it off

a cat won't go out
it sends its shadow instead
shadows can keep dry

rain so light so light
the black clouds must be holding
their own umbrellas

by the wet log pile
a new moon leans on my axe
fresh work—tomorrow

tea in the sukkah
more rain falls inside than out
songs are new raincoats

# Mexican Border, Detention Center

A butterfly sits on barbed wire
at the camp. A child claps her hands.
For the child, the wire flies away.
An inchworm inches forward,
measuring, as always, what's real
in a day. Other side of the fence,

---

ROGER NASH is inaugural poet laureate of the City of Greater Sudbury, and a past president of the League of Canadian Poets. Literary awards include the Canadian Jewish Book Award for Poetry, the PEN/O. Henry Prize Story Award, and being anthologized in *Best Canadian Poetry* (Biblioasis, 2020). His latest collection of poetry is *Climbing a Question* (Quattro Publishing, 2019).

coyotes sneeze behind a shed.
Wire and butterfly fly back.
The sky has no taste if you're hungry.
Ants come by on military parade.
Inchworm inches backwards, nothing
measured for sure. Soldiers fire
tear-gas again. The girl jumps,
taking flight like any butterfly.
She looks up: her parents are cloudlessly
blue today, wherever they took them.

# *Tikkun Olam*
## (the blitz of London)

The first sunbeams of the day
race into Grandma's kitchen without even
braking. So fast, with a conjuror's skill,
they seem not to be traveling at all.
But for her, nothing's allowed to shift
across geometry's etiquette of a table-setting
—until we sit down to eat:
cutlery and plates an exact pattern
of theorems that prove we're all still
here every morning – War or not.
Grandma's strict rules for kids
—"Don't scramble things more!"—put her
in charge even of laws of the cosmos:
sunbeams and a boy to be kept
in their places, until the time is right,
behind their respective high chairs.
She winks, so I know she quite understands:
kids are just the noisy part of light.
We, too, can help with *tikkun olam*.

# All the Broken Letters

*Sharon Dolin*

enter into a dance with
    the brokenness of me
        when I sit down to write
    to find a fullness in the words
I summon but can't control.

That's how I go on: bringing
    jagged edges of me—the badly
        begun, the woefully undone—
    to the edgy jags of letters
and through the thicket

of what gets composed,
    a path begins to clear
        toward you and the invisible
    one who contains all the letters
before they broke into song

then shattered from so much bright
    into bits floating like
        slow snow through the air
    of me onto the ground
of the page I am shaping

into words and phrases
    to send back up
into the aether once more.

SHARON DOLIN is the author of six books of poetry, most recently, *Manual for Living* (University of Pittsburgh Press, 2016). Her seventh book, *Imperfect Present,* is forthcoming from the University of Pittsburgh Press in *2022.* She is the author of a translation from Catalan of Gemma Gorga's *Book of Minutes* and a prose memoir, *Hitchcock Blonde* (Terra Nova Press, 2020). Winner of the Malinda A. Markham Translation Prize, her translation *Late to the House of Words: Selected Poems by Gemma Gorga* has just been published by Saturnalia Books. A 2021 NEA Fellowship recipient, she is associate editor of Barrow Street Press and directs Writing About Art in Barcelona.

# Listen to the quiet voice

underneath the hum of one
unbeknownst to you is the voice
that rides on the wind—

the one that feeds on the dusk's
last light, that pebble of bright
above rain cloud or snow

there is a brighter blue—stanchion
for all the horses you could never
corral or ride. Listen to the voice

after it has stopped speaking:
the words frame silences you
must now crane toward.

You are in that silence. So is God
knowing all unknowing. Listen
to the quiet and inside the glove

of muffled intent is a word
never before uttered
now flying in

with its speckled wings:
the contour you still seek
caught in the craw that soon sings.

# We Love the Red Bird Best

cardinal virtue    primary color
with his black eyes    black square beard
beneath his red beak
sitting on a branch of snow
what do we know    the new barred owl
that sits on a plane tree's

branch     the radius
of our walk condensed
to several blocks of masked light
we've moved far away
from the sun     our faith stolid
in its return     we spin ourselves
like a seasonal top     oh the flames
of blue inside the cooking fires of
the night     yellow will be the first
blossoms of spring     but here     early
winter     there are only the blessings
of birds     cantilevers of light
on stone     water-tower shadow thrown
against the wall     squirrel that hops inside
the tail of his shadow     we've grown heavy with
waiting for the dance dance
the bee inside the rose     only the cardinal
with his peaked red cap     to remind us
of winter's austere laugh.

# Sestina for a Body Art

*Mary Ellen Talley*

*You shall not make gashes in your flesh for the dead*
*nor incise any mark upon yourself*

Leviticus 19:28

If he were an observant Jew, it would be out of the question,
hints of Auschwitz numerology counted on the skin.
The tattoo artist turns to inform bystanders he doesn't need
faith to see the dark side. He wants his art and ink
penetrating dermal layers in shades of color,
circles shading inside outlines—tattoo machine moving
    forward.

If he were Jewish, his rabbi would say it's not moving
    forward—
mistaken decision should the artist ask the question,
but he won't. His millennial generation uses color
even on Shabbat, swirling strokes to pixilate layers of skin.
Traveling by sky, he hand-carries boxes of ink.
They are tools of his trade. Every artist will need

pigments—not to mar any body type, but to mark need.
He lets clients leaf through pages of flash until a forward
thrust of inspiration matches their intention. Stencil, then ink
correct spelling of a loved one and no one will question
the precision of fine lines, sharp poke of needle to skin,
repeat—repeat as the nondescript limb fills with color.

MARY ELLEN TALLEY's poems have recently been published in Banshee, Beir
Bua, The Plague Papers, and Ekphrastic Review as well as in the anthologies,
*Chrysanthemum* and *Take a Stand, Art Against Hate: A Raven Chronicles Anthology*.
Her poems have received three Pushcart nominations and her chapbook, *Postcards
from the Lilac City* was published by Finishing Line Press in 2020.

He is careful not to bleed the limb or smudge the color
partly because every design fulfills his own need.
He hones the craft for all who relish ornate skin,
his tool set at height to just pierce flesh is always moving
    forward.
At pain's onset, there is still time for skin to ask the question
why. The answer: one passion to wear intent and one to draw
    in ink.


The passion to draw on bodies begins with purchase of the ink,
then someone wanting permanent souvenir, or to wear color
of one's ethnicity. If asked, rabbis would likely nix the question
even if the body and the artist, both gentle rebels, need
and want to flow their intended beauty moving forward.
The artist with his earnest smile wears designs on his own skin.

A Jewish daughter sports *Chet*, *Zayin*, *Kuf*, strength adorning
    skin.
Other young Jews say their faith allows for anything in ink—
Star of David, or, in jest a *KOSHER* pig. Youth mixes back and
    forward.
One Jewish woman wears a hand of Miriam in deep blue color.
Biblical story prevents the rabbis from affirming, yes. They need
to maintain honor, the sordid histories of the question.

The artist argues the question is outdated. We're past taboos of
    skin.
His, the artist's need to express, as some desire to receive the
    flow of ink.
Shapes swirl color upon each body's body-part moving
    forward.

# In Greensboro

*Enid Shomer*

*For Ezell Blair, Jr. (Jibreel A-A. K-A. Khazan), Franklin McCain, Joseph McNeil, and David Richmond*

Woolworth's lunch counter, 1993*

This old downtown has slipped
into the historic sleep
that eventually turns
everything quaint: how people strolled
in the heat under the myopic
shade of wide-brimmed hats,
how they had their shoes shined
in step-up chairs, how the possibility
of justice startled us awake like light
striking film when four men
sat down here and waited to be served.

The lunch counter winds in sinuous
curves for maximum seating.
I'd hoped to find my heroes' pictures
or historic markers on the walls,
but photos of eggs and sausages,
laminated like diplomas,
provide the only Civics lesson
here: Man must eat. Still
something in me leaps this crisp March day,
for these brushed chrome bays
cordoned off now by a stripe of morning sun
like a period room in a museum,
or the scene of a crime as yet unsolved.

*A portion of the lunch counter is now preserved at the Smithsonian Museum.

ENID SHOMER's fifth collection of poetry, *Shoreless*, won the Lexi Rudnitsky Editor's Choice Award from Persea Books.

# Ascents

*Jay Yair Brodbar*

*As it were the very heaven for clearness.*

—Exodus 24:10

I.
Looking up, looking for that road,
sapphire-like, that God travels—
supernal breeze billowing
at the foot of the heavens.
Squinting into the blue, I cannot
distinguish among the myriad hues,
but for a very long time
my people have said:

*It is up there*

so I keep
searching.

II.
And God said:
*Come up to me on the mountain,*
*and be there.*

III.
And God showed all things
in one last breath on the last
mountain-top from which
Moses never again came down;
Moses, he had a promise
to pass on his wise breath.
And Joshua he trusted and touched
so that he, Joshua,
could also be carried
by that same sage wind.

JAY YAIR BRODBAR is a retired academic and Jewish communal executive. His poetry has appeared in *Parchment* and *McGill Street* among other publications.

IV.
*It is up there*

so I keep
searching.

# *Shechinah*

I.
As it was beginning there was
*Tohu Vavohu*

תהו ובהו

Some say:     *Unformed and void.*
Others say:   *Astonishingly empty.*
Some say:     *Welter and waste.*
Others say:   *There was wild howling.*

Undifferentiated, nebulous,
Barrenness.
Bewildering desolation.
Rashi says: *one would have been astonished and amazed at its
    emptiness.*

There was nothing.
As it was beginning, it was
Beginning with wild
Welter of waste,
Vacant tenebrous
Nothing.

II.
As it was beginning there was
Deep rushing waters.
Emptiness and unfathomable waters.
Unforgiving, muscular, darker-than-dark
Waters.

III.
And you descended.
Wind.
Breath.
Spirit.

Soul.
Presence.

Over the surface of the waters
You alighted,
Came near.

The book tenders:
*M'rachefet*

מרחפת

Some say:     *Hovered.*
Others say:   *Swept over.*
Some say:     *Swirled.*
Others say:   *Fluttered.*

The waters turned their face toward you.
You brushed close.
A skimmed caress.

# The Revolution of the Empty Sanctuary in Three Fictional Ancient Letters

*Rabbi Robert J. Ratner, PhD*

In memory and appreciation of our teacher Rabbi Dr. David B. Weisberg, *z"l*

I.
"Where is the god?"

To Milkilu
My husband
S  a  y:
Thus Anatilatu.
I am well.
May Ilu bless you
And make you well.

In Lachish, I entered
The sanctuary and
Brought the sheep and
The two jugs of oil
As you instructed me.
You said:
"Give it into the hand
Of the priest." I did (it).
You said:
"Watch the priest
When he places it
Before the god."

RABBI ROBERT J. RATNER, PhD (C88) is rabbi emeritus of Congregation Beth HaTephila, Asheville, North Carolina. He has published many articles on the Bible, biblical Hebrew grammar, and the Ancient Near East. He is a former editor of *Maarav* and co-editor of *The Stanley Gevirtz Memorial Volumes* (1992). He has served on the editorial board of the *CCAR Journal*, in which he has published an article, "Cain and Abel, and the Problem of Paradox" (1990), and two pieces of poetry.

I watched and, behold,
The priest placed it
Upon the altar.
But, my husband,
There is no god!
I said to the priest:
"Where is the god
To receive our offering?"
The priest said:
"The statue is no more.
God has received
The offering from my hand."

In the sanctuary
People look
This way
And people look
That way.
There is fear.
Please send word
That I may know
What to do.

II.*

"The sanctuary is empty."

*[This letter is moderately damaged. Restoration, where possible, is provided
in brackets.]

[To the ki]ng, my lord, say: Thus
[          ]mu, your servant. Seven
[And sev]en times I fall at the
[Feet of] the king, my lord.
May the king soon be well.

Your servant has written to his lord
About what he heard concerning
The sanctuary. As my lord
Commanded, I entered (it).
Behold, it is empty:
No statue, no image.

So I made inquiry
For the king, my lord. (It is) true.

The statue of the god
Was not stolen. None took it.

The Apiru removed it. They say:
"The statue will be destroyed!" and
Their priests say: "An image shall never
Again be set u[p        . . .         ]"

The sanctuary is empty. There [is no statu]e.
The ears of those who he[ar (it) ting]le.

The Apiru bring sh[eep an]d
The priests make off[erin]gs.
The king's sanctuary [is fil]led
With only smoke and ince[nse]
And song. Let Milkilu, my l[ord,]
Come when he recov[ers]
And see it for him[self].
(It is) true.

III.
"Is god in our midst or not?"

To Milkilu say:
Thus Anatilatu.
May Ilu return
Your strength.
(It is) bad here.

Your son found it.
Behind the sanctuary
In a garbage heap,
He found the god
You donated and
He said: "Below
The sculls of sheep and
Torn reed baskets
(Were) the god's feet,
Caked with oil and
Parched grain."
When he told me,
I asked the priest:
"What is this
That you have done?"

The men tear
Their clothing and
Throw ashes from
The garbage heap
Upon their heads.
They ask: "Is
God in our midst
Or not?" The women,
With their palms
Lifted to the Queen
Of Heaven, weep.

The priest said:
"Thus says Yah,
The god of the fathers:
'You must not mak[e . . . '" tablet broken]

# Ascension

*Rabbi Stephen S. Pearce, PhD*

Lethargy,
Weariness,
Huffing and puffing.
Chest pains.
Indigestion, he thinks,
But he has not eaten.

Mindlessly, he ascends, step by fatigued step
As if driven by interior gears,
Relieved of the pack
that grows smaller as he rises.
Not his worry anymore.
*I hope they make it*, he muses.

Deafening silence is welcome,
A portend of the end.
All he wants is rest.
And to have one final look
Across to the Land
He thinks he will not enter.

High on Nebo
Sky-blue-pink clouds
Touch the salty sea's wilderness's edge
And rise to the heights
Where Moriah comes into full view.
Clutching the taut fist that grabs his broken heart,

RABBI STEPHEN S. PEARCE, PhD (NY72) is senior rabbi emeritus and the Taube Emanu-El Scholar at Congregation Emanu-El of San Francisco. He is the author of *Flash of Insight: Metaphor and Narrative in Therapy* and served as the *CCAR Journal* editor from 2000 to 2003.

Squeezing tighter
He drops to his knees.
The world goes black against Moab's red rock.
His raiment sinks into the dust.
He is done,
Free to traverse the Jordan.

# *Havdalah*

## *Amy Bitterman*

I am the fertile octogenarian
The mother of a thousand twisty laws
When my son emerged
  blue and red and wet
  covered in a translucent veil of blood and love
I knew I'd given birth to my heart
I longed to call him Lev
But God and Man have long memories
And would not let me forget
  that I'd laughed when the
  angel told me I was pregnant
From the moment of his naming
Itzhak was his father's son
To name a thing is to own it

The double wick candle stands at attention
  in its golden holder
The spice box perfumes the air
  with nutmeg and cinnamon and myrrh
I stand ready to separate the holy from the mundane
  to cleave the sacred from the profane
But my husband and son are nowhere in sight
And the butcher knife is missing
A ripple of fear crosses my heart
when the angel appears
"It's all right," he/she says
  trailing light in his/her wake
"God has sacrificed a ram in your son's place"
He/she slaps his/her knee

AMY BITTERMAN has had short fiction accepted by *The Cream City Review, The Chicago Quarterly Review, The G.W. Review, The William and Mary Review, Switchback, The Literary Review, Kerem, Jewishfiction.net, The Crescent Review, Poetica, The Sand Hill Review, The Manhattanville Review, Emrys Journal, Folio,* and *Lilith.* In 2015, she was awarded a "Special Mention" for the Pushcart Prize. She currently teaches at Rutgers Law School.

"What a joke," he/she says
"What a rip snorter"

The match for the candle is struck and snuffed
           in the darkening tent
I wrap my cloak around my shoulders
           and walk into the sunset
Determined to console the mother of that ram

# The Whiteness of the Whale

*Rabbi James B. Rosenberg*

A half century ago—
    no, even more—
        Lawrence Ferlinghetti

Opened up the Coney Island
    of my Jewish mind
        though I could not know that
  then,

Taken, as I was, by those pictures of his gone world,
    a nearly naked lady
        hanging white sheet sails

On a harbor-side roof top, and Johnny Nolan
    running through screen door  summers
      with a patch on his ass,

And that calamitous one-night stand
    with the chick who, it turns out, hated poetry
      and had bad morning-after breath.

But what moves me now
    are those white spaces
      bathing his lines,

which tell me
    that the deepest freedom,
      the root of all expression,

---

In the fall of 2006, RABBI JAMES ROSENBERG completed a ten-year term as poetry editor of the *CCAR Journal*. In 2011 he published a collection of 121 of his poems, *Until the Blue Kingdom Comes.* He is a rabbi emeritus at Temple Habonim in Barrington, Rhode Island, has taught courses in Jewish studies at Tufts University and Connecticut College, and writes regular columns for the *Barrington Times* and *Jewish Rhode Island*.

lies not within the words  themselves,
        but within the white spaces
                in and around them,

Like the fiery force
        deep within the white spaces
                in and around the ink black Hebrew
                letters

Unfolding from right to left
        upon the worn parchment
                of a Torah scroll

Unfurled
        to catch the Divine Wind
                singing a sacred song

Of intimate and infinite

        silence.

# Call for Papers: *Maayanot*

The *CCAR Journal: The Reform Jewish Quarterly* is committed to serving its readers' professional, intellectual, and spiritual needs. In pursuit of that objective, the *Journal* created a new section known as *Maayanot* (Primary Sources), which made its debut in the Spring 2012 issue.

We continue to welcome proposals for *Maayanot* —translations of significant Jewish texts, accompanied by an introduction as well as annotations and/or commentary. *Maayanot* aims to present fresh approaches to materials from any period of Jewish life, including but not confined to the biblical or Rabbinic periods. When appropriate, it is possible to include the original document in the published presentation.

Please submit proposals, inquiries, and questions to *Maayanot* editor Rabbi Daniel F. Polish, dpolish@optonline.net.

Along with submissions for *Maayanot*, the *Journal* encourages the submission of scholarly articles in fields of Jewish studies, as well as other articles that fit within our Statement of Purpose.

The *CCAR Journal: The Reform Jewish Quarterly*
Published quarterly by the Central Conference of American Rabbis

Volume LXIX No. 1. Issue Number: Two hundred seventy

Winter 2022

## STATEMENT OF PURPOSE

The *CCAR Journal: The Reform Jewish Quarterly* seeks to explore ideas and issues of Judaism and Jewish life, primarily—but not exclusively—from a Reform Jewish perspective. To fulfill this objective, the *Journal* is designed to:

1. provide a forum to reflect the thinking of informed and concerned individuals—especially Reform rabbis—on issues of consequence to the Jewish people and the Reform movement;

2. increase awareness of developments taking place in fields of Jewish scholarship and the practical rabbinate, and to make additional contributions to these areas of study;

3. encourage creative and innovative approaches to Jewish thought and practice, based upon a thorough understanding of the traditional sources.

The views expressed in the *Journal* do not necessarily reflect the position of the Editorial Board or the Central Conference of American Rabbis.

The *CCAR Journal: The Reform Jewish Quarterly* (ISSN 1058-8760) is published quarterly by the Central Conference of American Rabbis, 355 Lexington Avenue, 8th Floor, New York, NY 10017. Application to mail at periodical postage rates is pending at New York, NY and at additional mailing offices.

Subscriptions should be sent to CCAR Executive Offices, 355 Lexington Avenue, 8th Floor, New York, NY 10017. Subscription rate as set by the Conference is $150 for a one-year subscription, $199 for a two-year subscription. Overseas subscribers should add $36 per year for postage. POSTMASTER: Please send address changes to *CCAR Journal: The Reform Jewish Quarterly,* c/o Central Conference of American Rabbis, 355 Lexington Avenue, 8th Floor, New York, NY 10017.

Typesetting and publishing services provided by Publishing Synthesis, Ltd., 39 Crosby Street, New York, NY 10013.

Copyediting services provided by Michael Isralewitz.

The *CCAR Journal: The Reform Jewish Quarterly* is indexed in the *Index to Jewish Periodicals.* Articles appearing in it are listed in the *Index of Articles on Jewish Studies* (of *Kirjath Sepher*) and in *Religious and Theological Abstracts.*

ISBN: 978-0-88123-617-0

# GUIDELINES FOR SUBMITTING MATERIAL

1.   The *CCAR Journal* welcomes submissions that fulfill its Statement of Purpose whatever the author's background or identification. Inquiries regarding publishing in the *CCAR Journal* and submissions for possible publication (including poetry) should be sent to the editor, Rabbi Elaine Rose Glickman, at journaleditor@ccarnet. org.

2.   Other than commissioned articles, submissions to the *CCAR Journal* are sent out to a member of the editorial board for anonymous peer review. Thus submitted articles and poems should be sent to the editor with the author's name omitted. Please use MS Word format for the attachment. The message itself should contain the author's name, phone number, and e-mail address, as well as the submission's title and a brief author biography.

3.   Books for review and inquiries regarding submitting a review should be sent directly to the book review editor, Rabbi Evan Moffic, at emoffic@gmail.com.

4.   Inquiries concerning or submissions for *Maayanot* (Primary Sources) should be directed to the *Maayanot* editor, Rabbi Daniel F. Polish, at dpolish@optonline.net.

5.   Based on Reform Judaism's commitment to egalitarianism, we request that articles be written in gender-inclusive language.

6.   The *Journal* publishes reference notes at the end of articles, but submissions are easier to review when notes come at the bottom of each page. If possible, keep this in mind when submitting an article. Notes should conform to the following style:

a. Rachel Adler, *Engendering Judaism: An Inclusive Theology and Ethics* (Philadelphia: Jewish Publication Society, 1999), 101–6. **[book]**

b. Lawrence A. Hoffman, "The Liturgical Message," in *Gates of Understanding*, ed. Lawrence A.Hoffman (New York: CCAR Press, 1977), 147–48, 162–63. **[chapter in a book]**

c. Richard Levy, "The God Puzzle," *Reform Judaism* 28 (Spring 2000): 18–22. **[article in a periodical]**

d. Adler, *Engendering,* 102. **[short form for subsequent reference]**

e. Levy, "God Puzzle," 20. **[short form for subsequent reference]**

f. Ibid., 21. **[short form for subsequent reference]**

7.   If Hebrew script is used, please include an English translation. If transliteration is used, follow the guidelines in the **Master Style Sheet**, available on the CCAR website at www.ccarnet.org.